Deanna J. Trakas (Ed.)

Focus Groups Revisted

MEDIZINKULTUREN IM VERGLEICH

MEDICAL CULTURES IN COMPARISON

herausgegeben von
edited by

Rolf Wirsing

und/and

Beatrix Pfleiderer

Band/Volume 22

LIT

Focus Groups Revisted

Lessons from qualitative research with children

edited by

Deanna J. Trakas

LIT

To the children who participated in the Living with Asthma in Childhood focus groups

Bibliographic information published by the Deutsche Nationalbibliothek
The Deutsche Nationalbibliothek lists this publication in the Deutsche Nationalbibliografie; detailed bibliographic data are available in the Internet at http://dnb.d-nb.de.

ISBN 978-3-8258-0041-3

A catalogue record for this book is available from the British Library

Verlagskontakt:
Fresnostr. 2 D-48159 Münster
Tel. +49 (0) 2 51/620 32 - 22 Fax +49 (0) 2 51/922 60 99
e-Mail: lit@lit-verlag.de http://www.lit-verlag.de

Auslieferung:

Deutschland/Schweiz: LIT Verlag Fresnostr. 2, D-48159 Münster
Tel. +49 (0) 2 51/620 32 - 22, Fax +49 (0) 2 51/922 60 99, e-Mail: vertrieb@lit-verlag.de

Österreich: Medienlogistik Pichler-ÖBZ GmbH & Co KG
IZ-NÖ, Süd, Straße 1, Objekt 34, A-2355 Wiener Neudorf
Tel. +43 (0) 2236/63 535-290, +43 (0) 2236/63 535 - 243, mlo@medien-logistik.at

Distributed in the UK by: Global Book Marketing, 99B Wallis Rd, London, E9 5LN
Phone: +44 (0) 20 8533 5800 – Fax: +44 (0) 1600 775 663
http://www.centralbooks.co.uk/html

Distributed in North America by:

Transaction Publishers
New Brunswick (U.S.A.) and London (U.K.)

Transaction Publishers
Rutgers University
35 Berrue Circle
Piscataway, NJ 08854

Phone: +1 (732) 445 - 2280
Fax: + 1 (732) 445 - 3138
for orders (U. S. only):
toll free (888) 999 - 6778
e-mail:
orders@transactionspub.com

Acknowledgements

I am indebted to the authors for waiting so patiently for their articles to appear in this volume and, with their trust, preserving the unity of our focus group with children adventure, which took place in six locations in Europe. Our coordination meetings, essential to the development of the procedures and resolution of issues described in the chapters to follow, were supported by the European Commission, BIOMED – Directorate General XII, with administrative assistance provided by the Institute of Child Health in Athens, Greece. The focus groups conducted during the *Living with Asthma in Childhood* project mobilized the resources of colleagues, junior scientists, nurses, teachers, and local authorities in a myriad of duties ranging from contacting children and their parents to arranging space for the sessions. I want to thank Emilio J Sanz for encouraging me to keep the manuscript for this book in perspective. Rolf Wirsing is especially appreciated for rejuvenating my attempts to make the book into an actuality which he carried forward in his creation of the camera-ready manuscript. One more time, I want to thank Sheena Nakou, paediatrician and perpetual sounding board throughout the project, for reviewing my initial editing of the chapters and having the fortitude to read several versions of the introductory and concluding chapters. Finally, a big, happy-face thank you is due to the children who took part in our focus groups and inspired us to rethink the basics and beyond.

Deanna J Trakas
Mytilini – Lesvos, Greece
October 2008

Contents

Foreword

Patricia J Bush

My introduction to focus group discussions with children began after nearly 20 years of experience with research about children's health behaviour and their needs for information about medicine use. The early studies were inspired by two questions I asked myself one day in the early 1970s while walking home from my office at Georgetown University School of Medicine in Washington, DC. First, "How old are children when they first have some responsibility for using medicines?"; followed by, "As with other health behaviors that children learn while under the supervision of others and then carry on independently, what should they know before they have that responsibility?" To answer my questions, I first looked for relevant literature. I found none. I then looked at school curricula for content about using medicines. All I found were "Don't do Drugs" and a few health education programmes for the prevention of poisoning in very young children. Thus, a pilot study in one elementary school was initiated to begin to learn what children of various ages did and believed relative to medicines (Bush and Davidson 1982). It led to larger studies in Washington, DC, schools (Bush et al. 1985), followed by an invitation to join the United States Pharmacopeia (USP) as a Visiting Scholar to develop a children and medicines programme.

At USP, I initiated a multidisciplinary expert panel whose members soon recommended that we find out what children wanted to know about medicines in addition to what they did and believed. These three areas – behaviors, beliefs, and perceived needs for information – seemed crucial to investigate before any attempts were undertaken to develop health education programmes about medicines for children. This eventually led to my introduction to focus group discussions with schoolchildren, but only after a long experience with questionnaire-based research during which I became well-aware of the limitations of using closed-answer questionnaires. In particular, anticipating the range of children's possible answers was always a central problem as illustrated by the following example – and I challenge even the most experienced questionnaire specialist to be able to anticipate the final answer of this third grader to a questionnaire which provided five response options from "not likely" to "very likely":

> How likely is it that you have trouble sleeping?
> Very likely.
> When you have trouble sleeping, how likely are you to take something special for it?
> Very Likely.
> When you take something special for trouble sleeping, what do you take?
> A teddy bear.

I had also learned to be very careful about asking "yes—no" questions. For example, before administering a Health Locus of Control Scale to schoolchildren, we wanted to make sure that they understood how to indicate their "yes" or "no" answers using the scale's graphics, so our research team went through some sample questions. We asked a young student, "Did you ride an elephant to school today?" She pointed to the "yes" answer. We then asked, "How did you know?" She quickly replied, "The elephant told me."

Following our work on children's health beliefs and behaviors relative to medicines, we decided to focus on what children wanted to know about them. We decided that focus groups would be the most efficient way for us to learn about these matters. In the early 1990s, we found very little scientific literature about children's focus groups to guide us – very similar to the situation the contributors to this book encountered a few years later when they began the *Living with Asthma in Childhood* project (ASPRO2). Based on the recommendations of Debus (1995) and our collaborative experiences in working with children, we developed our own interview guide which we used for conducting focus groups in three school systems in the USA (Menacker et al. 1999).

In 1996, I was asked to join ASPRO2 as project consultant and to train the research team members in focus group methods. This was a continuation of my collaboration in two previous multidisciplinary concerted actions, under the same project coordination, supported by the European Commission. Because of our experience with children in the series of US studies, we had been invited to participate in the projects and I coordinated the US local research teams. The COMAC Childhood and Medicines Project involved healthy children and their families in ten research locations (Bush et al. 1996, Trakas and Sanz 1992, 1996). The second was concerned with the investigation of the socio-cultural and pharmacological management of asthma in childhood (ASPRO1). Both projects used qualitative research methods developed specifically for use with children – in particular the drawing-interview and a semi-structured fever interview.

The reasons to use focus groups in health education programmes with children are basically the same as those for using them with adults. They are useful 1) prior to developing a survey instrument when the range of possible questions and answers is unknown and the survey will be administered to a large population thus limiting probing and open-ended responses, 2) when educational materials are being developed and, 3) when educational materials are being evaluated. Focus groups might be used at a number of stages in one educational research project; for example, in one study they were used before and during the development of a health education CD-ROM for children with leukemia (Dragone et al. 2002). Children with the disease and their families were involved in the focus groups before the CD was made and later it was pilot-tested in another set of focus groups.

The ASPRO2 focus groups were performed in the context of a multi-sited study about the life experiences of children with asthma and their perceived needs for information; e.g., how they live with asthma, what they want to know about their own care, what concerns or interests them aside from their asthma. One of the goals of the project was to obtain information that could be directed towards better health education of these children and their experiences with existing programmes such as camping with other children with asthma, and special "asthma and allergies day" activities. An animated cartoon asthma education video shown at the beginning the session was intended to stimulate discussion.

The focus group literature usually recommends that participants be as similar as possible, a suggestion that was followed by ASPRO2 coordinators in planning sessions which controlled for age, gender, and severity of asthma. However, controlling for the homogeneity of cultural factors was a challenge for the project which performed focus groups in six European locations: the Canary Islands and mainland Spain, Finland, Germany, Great Britain and Greece. In addition, differences among the research teams led to variations in focus group styles. While the Finnish and German teams strictly followed the moderator's guide protocol, the team in the Canary Islands developed a series of games, targeted for use among the 6 to 8 year-olds, based on the thematic points in the moderator's guide. The other three teams followed the project's formal focus group format; particularly with the youngest groups, some allowed longer periods of warm-up games or breaks, or added role-playing activities to enhance discussion. The options in formats and styles discussed in this volume provide inside information (e.g., differences in motivation, rationale, and content) which can be helpful to other researchers in selecting which mode is best suited for the groups of children in their investigations.

One strategy that has been repeatedly demonstrated as successful in promoting discussion is highly recommended for focus groups with children – the use of stimulus materials. In our US study in three school systems (Menacker et al. 1999), we used empty packages of common medicines as stimulus materials. One of our collaborators tried focus groups without the medicine packages and found that it was very difficult to get the children to talk about medicines compared to groups where the packages were used. This was also the experience of Katri Hämeen-Anttila who was not allowed to use medicine packages in her focus groups in Finland and found it very difficult to get the children to discuss medicines (Hämeen-Anttila 2006, et al. 2006). In ASPRO2, aside from the cartoon video, stimulus materials were provided by games, particularly those used by the local team in the Canary Islands; for example, over-sized dice with questions and commands printed on the faces, a grab-bag with various asthma-related objects which were used to create narratives.

For scientists interested in the application of research to health education programmes and materials, an important question concerns whether the results of ASPRO2 were different or similar enough to serve as the basis for asthma education materials that could be adapted to local situations. Were the purposes in each locale the same; were the outcomes the same? Although beyond the scope of this book, for future multi-site focus group research, it would be informative if different methods were tried in the same research location among similar groups of children and their outcomes compared. Limited experience suggests that similar methods can result in similar results in very different countries or societies. The results of school-based questionnaires administered to children in Armenia, Malaysia, Nepal, and the USA concluded that it is quite feasible for a common medicines education programme to be developed for application in different societies which would need only minor adaptations to local practices (Bush and Joshi 2002; Bush et al. 1996).

After decades of studies about children's needs for information about medicines (Hämeen-Anttila and Bush 2008), it is extremely gratifying that the national health policy of some countries, such as Finland, have mandated teaching schoolchildren about medicines as an obligatory school subject. The results of focus groups conducted with schoolchildren were used to develop the curriculum which is available free of charge via the internet[1] and users are free to adapt it to their local situations. Wouldn't it be nice if information obtained via focus groups from children with asthma could form the basis of asthma education programs which would be available on the internet and adaptable to local situations? The first step in reaching this goal might be to concentrate on learning more about focus groups with children – a good reason to explore the contents of the volume with imagination and an appreciation of the possibilities.

Endnote

[1] The site for obtaining the health education package for teaching children about medicines in the school curriculum: www.uku.fi/medicinescurriculum

References

Bush PJ and Davidson FR 1982. Medicines and "drugs": What do children think? *Health Education Quarterly* 9:113-128. Reprinted 1989 in *Children's Health Beliefs and Behaviors*, DS Gochman and GS Parcel (eds). Human Sciences Press, New York. Abstracted 1989 in *Pharmacy Practice: Social and Behavioral Aspects, 3rd edn.* MC Smith and AI Wertheimer (eds). University Park, Baltimore.

Bush PJ, Iannotti RJ, Davidson FR 1985. A longitudinal study of children and medicines. In *Topics in Pharmaceutical Sciences*, DD Breimer and P Speiser (eds). Elsevier Sciences Publications.

Bush PJ, Trakas DJ, Sanz EJ, Wirsing RL, Vaskilampi T, Prout A (eds) 1996. *Children, Medicines, and Culture.* Pharmaceutical Products Press, Binghamton, NY.

Bush P and Joshi M 2002. Towards a universal curriculum for teaching children about medicines. Paper presented at the Federation Internationale Pharmaceutique World Congress, Nice, France 31 Aug-5 Sept.

Debus M 1995. *Methodological Review: a Handbook for Excellence in Focus Group Research.* Academy for Educational Development, Washington, DC.

Dragone MA, Bush PJ, Jones JK, Kamani S 2002. Development and evaluation of an interactive CD-ROM for children with leukemia and their families. *Patient Education and Counseling* 46(4):297-301.

Hämeen-Anttila K 2006. *Education Before Medication: Empowering children as medicine users.* Unpublished doctoral dissertation, Department of Social Pharmacy, Faculty of Pharmacy, University of Kuopio.

Hämeen-Anttila K, Juvonen M, Ahonen R, Bush PJ, Airaksinen M 2006. How well can children understand medicine related topics? *Patient Education and Counseling* 60:171–178.

Hämeen-Anttila K and Bush PJ 2008. Healthy children's perceptions of medicines: a review. *Research in Social and Administrative Pharmacy* 4(2):985-1114.

Menacker F, Aramburuzabala P, Minian N, Bush PJ, Bibace R 1999. Children and medicines: What they want to know and how they want to learn. *Journal of Social and Administrative Pharmacy* 16:38-52.

Trakas DJ and Sanz EJ (eds) 1992. *Studying Childhood and Medicine Use.* ZHTA Medical Publications, Athens.

Trakas DJ and Sanz EJ (eds) 1996. *Childhood and medicine use in a cross-cultural perspective: a European concerted action.* European Commission, Directorate-General, Science, Research and Development, Luxembourg.

Introduction
An invitation to visit children's focus groups

Deanna J Trakas

The new directions in the sociology and anthropology of childhood which emerged in the late 1980s invited theoretically and methodologically innovative approaches to conducting research with children. Following in close chronological synchronization, by the 1990s the merits of qualitative research about health issues had begun to receive recognition in "certain circles", such as health policy planning and health promotion, where focus groups were also enjoying considerable popularity. In this rapidly changing time frame, the *Living with Asthma in Childhood* project (ASPRO2) was launched in 1996 with the generous support of the European Commission Directorate General XII (BIOMED) for Science, Research and Development[1]. This was the final project in a package of three consecutive European concerted actions which aimed to develop and refine qualitative methodologies for research with children about their perceptions of illness and medicines. The first two projects concentrated on techniques for use at the individual level (Trakas & Sanz 1992, Trakas & Sanz 1996, Bush et al. 1996); in the third, it was the focus group which occupied centre stage.

All the pieces of a successful blueprint seemed to be in place, except for one: The protocol for focus groups at the time was created around adult participants – usually from mainstream, western social categories. We needed to edit the script and develop child-centred strategies. As we followed the task we were able to observe the practical and methodological issues which arise when focus groups are moved out of their "home territory", transferred across boundaries and used with new social collectivities. The process is documented in the chapters of this book, perhaps the only set of commentaries which is the result of a single-project coordinated effort to implement focus groups with children.

Research Background for the Collection

Before introducing the chapters, a short discussion of the context of the *Living with Asthma in Childhood* project is presented. The intention is to set the framework for "revisiting" – an idea which may acquire new meanings as focus groups are moved out of their traditional settings and concepts such as empowerment, intersubjectivity and solidarity are interjected into the terrain. As an archive of experience or as a text of the times, the collection of articles revisits the process of applying the focus group prototype with children: First, at the level of simple practicalities and secondly, in a space where differences in settings (cultural, environmental, physical) create new discourses about focus groups. This, in turn, serves as a mirror for reflecting upon recurring issues about the focus group discussion as a qualitative technique and methodological concept.

Conducting focus groups, or perhaps the appropriate expression would be *performing in* them, rests on the capabilities of the researchers ("moderators") to inspire and facilitate interaction between the participants. Conversation and chatting is usually considered to be an essential part of adult behaviour; thus, focus group discussions are assumed to be based on a natural event and normalized for all social categories. Handbooks explaining the technique, which began to circulate in the late-1980s, often suggested that, in the event that focus groups would be conducted with children, *modifications* might be necessary (Krueger 1988, Morgan 1988, 1993, Stewart and Shadansani 1990). The need for possible changes in focus group protocol usually rests on cautions about differences in children's developmental levels, especially the "problem" of working around the "short attention span". The idea of modifications indicates (perhaps unwittingly) that the norm is the adult group; the children's focus group, an engineered variety.

The same messages, without much new elaboration, continue to appear in updated editions of the original handbooks (e.g., Kennedy et al. 2001, Krueger and Casey 2000, Morgan 1997). Market researchers had seized the opportunity early on to implement focus groups with children beginning in the 1980s (e.g., McDonald and Topper 1988, Spethman 1992, Winski 1992) – but it seemed that their results-driven approach left little room for theorizing about children's communication patterns or appreciating the ethical issues entailed in bringing children together to talk with a moderator – usually an adult stranger. Until the mid-1990s, scientists intending to conduct focus groups with children found themselves in a methodological vacuum and even the practical matters could only be imagined. The lack of child-centred "how-to" focus group handbooks served as an impetus for organizing this collection which is based the coordination manual we developed for ASPRO2.

The re-theorizing about children and childhood from anthropology and sociology in the 1990s challenged the extant orthodox developmental paradigms and childhood socialization theory (Alanen 1992, Anderson 1996, James 1993, James and Prout 1990, James et al. 1998, Holloway and Valentine 2000, Mayall 1994a&b). Children are no longer to be viewed as passive vessels waiting to be filled by adult images of maturity; as plastic to be moulded by grown-ups, as apprentices to adults or works in progress. They are social actors in their own right and active agents in their acquisition of social skills; a view completely compatible with new conventions about children's rights which make it imperative that their voices be included in research about matters affecting them [2]. It is probably not a coincidence that concerns about the theoretical and ethical issues of children's focus groups began to appear late in the 1990s (e.g., Baker R et al. 1996, Green and Hart 1999, Horowitz et al 2003, Menacker et al. 1999, Mitchell 1999).

The similarities between the issues which were problematized during ASPRO2 and those addressed in the recent literature indicate a need for creating a discourse about children's focus groups from a wider, comparative research base. The parallels between the suggestions in this volume and those in the 2002 article by Myfanwy Morgan and Nicky Britten are to be expected; they were the national coordinators for the ASPRO2 local study in Great Britain (M Morgan et al. 2002). The methodological concerns raised by Katri Hämeen-Anttila and her colleagues in social pharmacy in Finland (2006) and by Faith Gibson from nursing in Great Britain (2007) coincide with a number of points discussed in the chapters in this volume. Even though they were drafted a few years before these most recent publications, the chapters are both contemporary as well as representing an archive of earlier experience.

During a decade when both qualitative health research and anthropological perspectives on childhood were in their formative stages, funding at the level of the European Union came as an unexpected encouragement. From the experience of the two previous concerted actions, our sense of continuity and cohesiveness had grown; our scientific directions and communicative purposefulness had solidified. The diversity in our scientific disciplines led to a productive dialogue between qualitative and quantitative approaches, bringing conceptualizations and terms of reference into close proximity. Differences in our cultural backgrounds contributed to a collage of understandings about children from different European regions and pinpointed variations in national policies and local adaptations to ethical issues in qualitative research with youth. Our different levels of research experience, ranging from undergraduate student to junior scientists to professors, created a need for egalitarian interactions and flexible consensus-building strategies. In the earlier projects we had concentrated on developing and refining data collection and analysis techniques designed for individual interaction as well as specifically for children; in particular, the "drawing-interview" to elicit children's narratives about illness experiences and discuss the role they assign to medicines, and the "fever interview", a more goal-oriented instrument which lent itself to greater opportunities for cross-cultural comparisons (Bush et al. 1996, Trakas 1992, Wirsing and Trakas 1996a&b, Trakas & Sanz 1992, 1996). In the third project, we turned our attention to the development of methods to explore children in collectivities through the use of focus groups, a technique originally not designed with children in mind, but one which we would re-create for them.

With the above as a backdrop, we began preparation for ASPRO2. A few points in the early planning stages which are not addressed in the chapters are worth mentioning here. First, our focus group training seminar conducted by Ron Iannotti (Iannotti and Bush 1992) and Pat Bush (see Foreword, this volume) included role-playing in "mock" sessions with members assigned to act as moderators as well as participant stereotypes (e.g., shy, chatty, hostile, disruptive, hyperkinetic). While this type of exercise helped to create an idea of what a focus group "looks like", the chance to play naughty children was all too tempting an invitation to even the most serious scientists in our group. As a consequence, perhaps, we were pre-occupied with the notion of "maintaining discipline" during the planning stages; a concern which, in practice, was exaggerated.

Second, we felt quite enthusiastic about having located a cartoon video about asthma, produced by a pharmaceutical company for children and available in all of the countries in the project. We considered the "Oscar" video, (our term of reference) as ideal for use as an entry point in the focus group discussion and for the foundation of standardizing the moderator's guide. The guide for the focus group format was piloted in two locations and with the revised version in hand, we set out to begin the main investigation: Emilio Sanz and Marcellino Garcia in Tenerife, Spain; Pilar Aramburuzabala and Maria Vega in Madrid; Rolf Wirsing and Annette Drews in Goerlitz, Germany; Tuula Vaskilampi and Outi Hallia in Kuopio, Finland; Nicky Britten and Myfanwy Morgan in London, Great Britain; myself in Greece. We were joined by our local team members who brought a unique identity to the study in each site, also reflected in the articles in this collection.

Organization of the Collection

Each chapter in this volume addresses a dimension of focus groups which provoked repeated discussion, even heated debate, during the project. Some emerged as a result of specific theoretical interests and practical orientations of local teams; others were inspired by the need to elaborate existing guidelines, not only to make focus groups children-specific, but to reconsider the basic assumptions which formed the technique's foundations. The first two articles discuss communicative behaviours among children, one from an anthropological perspective, the other from developmental psychology theory. Both viewpoints have implications for moderator preparation, a topic addressed specifically in the third article. The fourth and fifth articles examine the geography of focus groups; gaining access to participants, getting them to the focus group location, creating child-friendly focus group environments. The issue of ethics appears most clearly in the process of "recruiting", but ethical concerns are interwoven into all phases of focus group research. The next pair of articles, essentially continuing with the context of the geography and ethics of focus groups, offers a contrast between two models for conducting groups with children; a structured format for traditional methods for facilitating discussion and a game-playing approach. The final article in the original series suggests possible ways to develop methods of analysis for focus group content, especially for dimensions of interaction in collectivities. The concluding article, written a few years after the other chapters had been edited (in 2004), aims to synthesize a methodological problematic which takes into account historical contexts, conceptual frameworks and theoretical underpinnings of focus group research.

In his charming chapter about children's communication, Michael Anderson, consultant to ASPRO2, proposes that the focus group is potentially an ethnographic event; however, he expresses concern that they often tend to be contrived, rather than naturally unfolding social happenings. As a result, according to Anderson, it would be "erroneous to assume that the interaction and knowledge generated in a focus group is pure, authentic and natural." Researchers need to be aware of the intent of the focus group as well as the possibility that the participants, particularly when they are children, may have interpretations of the purpose of the discussion very different from those of the researchers. Pretence, conformity, compliance and silence, characteristics of communication present in most focus groups, are explored within the framework of children's interactions. Anderson interweaves these elements with the hegemony inherent in focus groups, questioning the notion that they could be used as a means of "empowerment" for the participants. The strategies of social interaction and the risks involved in discussion are factors which may impede or enhance the egalitarian goals of these groups.

The topic of communication with and between children is continued by Maria Vega and Pilar Aramburuzabala, the coordinators of the Madrid team which was composed of child psychologists and pedagogues. Their article addresses the repeated advisories of focus group manuals which priorities the need for information about children's developmental levels and psychosocial capabilities when planning, implementing and analyzing children's focus groups. Beyond their elaboration of this much needed information, however, the authors point out that what children say and do is often a reflection of their parents' world view and behaviours, and may not represent their own thoughts and feelings. As educators and developmental psychologists, the authors were concerned that children can be particularly susceptible to pleasing their elders, especially when they meet a new adult (such as a focus group moderator) in a new situation. Indeed, while most adults in the western world have heard references to focus groups in casual conversation and have at least a vague idea that discussion is central to the exercise; children usually do not have this exposure. Even if they have heard the term, the idea of a focus group probably is of no interest to them; e.g., It would be unexpected for children to be heard saying that they are going to be part of a focus group with any enthusiasm.

Conducting focus groups with specific social categories of participants requires knowledge about their shared culture and perceptions of discussion etiquette. While anthropologists tend to view childhood developmental theory as a-cultural, it is important in sorting out linguistic capabilities and social interaction. Researchers are reluctant to adopt qualitative methods for use with children; they see children as less competent and less social than adults. Part of the issue about competency seems to relate to doubts about children's ability to talk about "reality" (instead of "fantasy"), which further implicates the "problem of honesty". Strangely enough (or not), questions about reality and honesty rarely come up as reservations about the "data produced" in adult focus groups. It is not by chance that modifications which might be necessary for children's focus groups continue to emphasize the need to look towards developmental level theories as the major instrument to guide moderators. The dimension of multiple realities is central in interactive research strategies, independent of age.

The imagination is easily captured by the vision of focus groups as lively events full of interaction between participants who (although initially strangers to each other) present conflicting opinions, engage in debate, resolve differences and reach a consensus; and, in the process, "produce data". Compared to group interviews where the research remains visible throughout, the focus group moderator is expected to fade into the periphery. The metamorphosis is easier to achieve when the group is relatively homogeneous, the image of the moderator. When moderators are clearly quite different from the rest of the participants, slipping into the sidelines of the group interaction is probably wishful thinking. The vision becomes blurred when the technique is introduced to a social category of people unfamiliar to the moderator (or vice versa); here the "role of" the moderator (as a sensitive but structured facilitator) may be less important than, for example, understandings about the communicative behaviours of, for example, the elderly, "ethnicities", youth, children.

"Good moderators" are often described in terms of their exceptional communication skills demonstrated by a near-innate talent to put others at ease, project acceptance of others, convey warmth and awareness of their personal body language. In the third chapter, Annette Drews asks, "Where do you find a 'saint' like this for focus groups in general and more particularly for those with children?" In response to her own question, Drews developed and implemented a training programme to increase moderator competency for the local study in Goerlitz. While her immediate goal was to train social work students for the ASPRO2 research with children's focus groups, her methods are applicable for moderators working with other age groups. Techniques to assist moderator relaxation, concentration, and self-discovery, and enhance communication skills are described in the article along with the students' evaluations of the training. This approach certainly puts things in a different light; for example, moderators may be extremely well-versed in children's developmental levels and intellectually enlightened about the sociocultural characteristics of the participant groups in their research, but may not be at ease with themselves. Children may sense the resulting discomfort of the moderator which can influence their own feelings of ease and security in the focus group.

The importance of selecting and training moderators is emphasized in virtually all focus group manuals; often, more weight is given to the selection of moderators, less to training techniques. For example, moderators should be selected according to their identification with or existing knowledge about the social group of people who will participate in their focus groups; e.g., gender, age, immigrant experience, minority affiliation, and other indicators of homogeneity. According to this rationale, moderators of children's focus groups should either be quite young themselves or selected from professions which train people to "feel comfortable" with and "know how to talk to children"; for example, school teachers, child psychologists, paediatric nurses, or parents. This overlooks that the role of the moderator in focus groups is not a matter of "talking to", but rather facilitating interaction between the participants and listening to what they say. Further, being a teacher or parent does not ensure competency in talking with children or ability to conform to the role assigned to them in the research protocol. Specialists, as they become socialized by their academic field and experience, can acquire stereotypic or rigid ways of interacting with children; for example, long-term primary school teachers with didactic devices used to instil knowledge, might resort to these skills in focus groups and appear that they are testing the children. After many years in the classroom or in the paediatric clinic the "teacher", "nurse" or "caregiver" persona shows through.

Based on the experience with the Goerlitz study, Rolf Wirsing's chapter about locating children, inviting them to participate, arranging times and places and generally forming focus groups was initially intended to be straightforward and utterly practical. His attention to a variety of details, with wide-ranging implications, provides a perfect example of how exploring even the most basic mechanics of the adult protocol and apply it to children can result in a re-assessment of the entire focus group enterprise. As he points out, "Most methods for locating and recruiting adults for focus groups are unsuitable for children", which eventually places the topic of "recruitment" squarely in the arena of qualitative research ethics. Gaining access to children as potential participants is ethically sensitive; for example, collaborating with schools or clinics for rosters of children's names brings up a series of confidentiality issues. The scheduling of children's groups is dependent on not only the potential participant's programme, but on that of others as well; tutors, extra-curricular activities, parent's shopping plans, and so on. Issues of safety (and liability) arise with plans for independent transport of children to group sites. Thus, the geography of children's focus groups suggests a series of intricate ethical considerations are automatically brought under scrutiny, some relevant to all focus group research but perhaps overlooked.

The physical environment can promote children's feelings of well-being and enhance their enjoyment of participation in the focus group. The article of Topalidou, Menaxiadi and Trakas continues the discussion of focus group geography by reviewing the variety of approaches to creating ambiance by the local ASPRO2 teams, with respect not only to the focus group room itself, but also to the characteristics of the peripheral or exterior area. Placing focus groups in schools or hospitals, geographies loaded with explicit and implicit adult-child power relations, may have an effect on children's consent or assent; voluntariness may be compromised (Abramovitch et al. 1991) and children may be hesitant to express the desire to drop-out once the group has begun (Miller & Nelson 2006). While hospitals were used in some of the local studies, the focus group rooms and even the access to them were purposely located away from clinical facilities. Classrooms sometimes offered minimal potential for re-arranging desks and chairs, while multi-use rooms offered greater flexibility for alternative seating arrangements using exercise mats and large pillows on the floor to help to minimize the moderator-children "distance". When the characteristics of the room allowed children to move around and change seating arrangements, greater interaction between them resulted. Although this geography renders seating charts obsolete (the standard recommended procedure from adult focus group manuals), it was a positive and balanced trade-off.

It is fitting that the article about designing focus group formats is authored by Outi Hallia and Tuula Vaskilampi, as it was their Kuopio team which piloted the initial format, along with Rolf Wirsing and Annette Drews from the Goerlitz team. They were central in the process of incorporating revisions into the final format and writing the accompanying moderator's guide which included a set of detailed instructions for each step in the format and a "worksheet" chart to coordinate the content of the audio tape with the notations of the assistant moderator. The format began with suggestions for introducing the moderators to the group and warm-up activities to familiarize the participants with each other. Following the viewing of the "Oscar" video, the discussion began with four recall questions about the content of the video. A series of themes for exploration completed the format. Differences in the application of the format by the local research teams are discussed, including the addition of role-playing activities and the deletion of the video viewing. The article concludes with the consideration that cultural variations may contribute to the way in which the format is used; for example, as a complete package or as a flexible set of suggestions. While the video of the 1980s looked good on paper as a standardized stimulus material, we found that it did not work so well in the real world of the children of the 1990s.

The Tenerife team, spearheaded by a group of creative teachers-in-training decided to dispense not only with the "Oscar" video, but the entire notion of a traditional, structured format. With the approval of their study coordinator, a clinical pharmacologist who nevertheless was quickly convinced that game-playing would make things much more interesting for everyone, they developed a repertoire of game materials which incorporated all of the ASPRO2 focus group format themes. In the eighth article in this volume, Emilio Sanz reviews the rationale of his team for creating the game-playing strategy, pointing out its foundations in (adult) focus group repertoires, including the concept of stimulus materials. Warm-up introductories were assisted by the distribution of t-shirts printed with the logo of the project and *Tengo asthma – soy feliz*! (I have asthma – I'm fine!), and worn by both the children and the moderators. The article outlines the procedures for using the game materials; for example, a rendition of a table game was enlarged to cover a sizable floor space and included a package of cards with questions and role-playing options. A more modest set of materials consisted of two large dice, with similar questions and role-playing options on each of the six faces. The creation of focus groups as "happenings" of game-playing and "incentive" gifts to children raises a series of methodological and ethical questions about expanding the boundaries of the focus group model and the selection of incentive objects.

The analysis of focus groups in the 1990s was somewhat of a mystery to novice moderators and other researchers involved in harvesting and processing information produced by participants. The issues which preoccupied the members of ASPRO2 parallel those which appeared in the literature of the decade. In addition, we were under an essentialist illusion throughout most of the project that the technique is a tightly bounded entity, governed by strict rules which define it. If either the boundaries or the rules were to be bent at any point of the procedures (synthesis of groups, data collection, analysis), we imagined that our focus groups would become something else – as game-playing events or ... un-focused group discussions. Focus groups can serve different purposes; consequently, analysis should conform to the trajectory of the goals rather than insist on the purity of (yet-to-be-established) analytical orthodoxies. The analysis of academic focus groups need not be results-driven in the tradition of market research – and analytical tools need to be selected with an eye of process (rather than findings only). Potentials for analyzing focus groups as if they are ethnographic phenomena need exploration – and potentials for developing analytical methods specifically designed for focus groups remains a challenge. The ninth article in this book, provided by myself (Trakas), reviews these issues in greater detail, offering examples from project-level experience and approaches of the Greek local team.

The final chapter was drafted after a significant period of time had passed following the end of the project and after the initial editing of the other chapters. What began as a short epilogue grew in response to the considerable flurry of activity to move academic focus groups into new sociocultural territories and experiment with their capacities among different types of people. Introducing focus groups to children was probably the first major effort to use the technique in a new social collectivity. A parallel expansion of focus groups was underway as they were taken into health care research, an area very compatible with market research; for example, the patient as consumer of medical services and technological products. More recently, the focus group agenda is gaining attention for its potential to empower the participants and create solidarity between them. From the viewpoint of the sociology of knowledge, the focus group is a clear example of how the tempo of the times shapes research methodologies.

Endnotes

[1]European Commission Directorate General XII for Science, Research and Development (BIOMED), Contract #BMH4-CT96-066

[2]Paraphrasing from Article 12 of the 1989 United Nations Convention of the Rights of the Child: children have a right to be involved in decisions that affect them as individuals and as a collectivity.

References

Abramovitch R, Freedman J, Thoden K, Nikolich C 1991. Children's capacity to consent to participation in psychological research: empirical findings. *Child Development* 62:1100–1109.

Alanen L 1992. Modern Childhood: Exploring the "child question" in sociology. *Research Report 50*. University of Jyvaskyla, Finland.

Anderson M 1996. Childhood, Culture and Identity, Unpublished Ph.D Thesis, University of Hull.

Baker R, Panter-Brick C et al. 1996. Methods used in research with children in Nepal. *Childhood* 3 (2): 171-193. [Special issue "Children out of Place", M Connolly and J Ennew (eds.)]

,

Bush PJ, Trakas DJ, Sanz EJ, Wirsing RL, Vaskilampi T, Prout A (eds) 1996. *Children, Medicine and Culture.* Haworth (Pharmaceutical Products Press), Binghamton NY.

Gibson F 2007 Conducting focus groups with children and young people: Strategies for success. *Journal of Research in Nursing* 12:473-483.

Green J and Hart L 1999. The impact of context on data. In: Developing Focus Group Research: Politics, Theory and Practice, RS Barbour and J Kitzinger (eds). Sage, London.

Hämeen-Anttila K, Juvenen M, Ahonen R, Bush PJ, Airaksinen M 2006. How well can children understand medicine related topics? *Patient Education and Counseling* 60:171-178.

Holloway S and Valentine G 2000. Children's geographies and the new social studies of childhood. In: *Children's Geographies: Playing, living, learning.* S Holloway and G Valentine (eds). Routledge, London.

Horowitz J, Vessy J, Carlson K, Bradley J, Montoya C, McCullough B 2003. Conducting school-based focus groups: lessons learned from the Cats Project. *Journal of Pediatric Nursing* 18(5):321-331.

Iannotti RJ and Bush PJ 1992. The development of autonomy in children's health behaviour. In *Emotion, Cognition, Health, and Development in Children and Adolescents*, EJ Sussman, LV Feagans and W Ray (eds). Earlbaum, Englewood Cliffs NJ.

James A 1993. *Childhood Identities: Self and social relationships in the life of the child.* Edinburgh University Press, Edinburgh.

James A and Prout A (eds) 1990. *Constructing and Deconstructing Childhood.* Falmer Press, Basingstroke.

James A, Jenks C, Prout A (eds) 1998. *Theorizing Childhood.* Polity Press, London.

Kennedy C, Kools S, Krueger R 2001. Methodological considerations in children's focus groups. Nursing Research 50(2):184-187.

Krueger RA 1988. *Focus Groups: A practical guide for applied research* (with a foreward by Michael Quinn Patton). Sage, Newbury Park.

Krueger R and Casey M 2000. *Focus Groups: A practical guide for applied research.* Sage Publications, Thousand Oaks California.

Mayall B 1994a. *Negotiating Health: School children at home and at school.* Cassell, London.

Mayall B 1994b. *Children's Childhoods: Observed and experiences.* Falmer, London.

McDonald WJ and Topper GE 1988. Focus group research with children: A structural approach. Applied Marketing Research 28:3-11.

Menacker F, Aramburuzabala P, Minian N, Bush PJ, Bibace R 1999.Children and medicines: What they want to know and how they want to learn. *Journal of Social and Administrative Pharmacy*, 18(1): 38-52.

Miller VA and Nelson RM 2006. A developmental approach to child assent for nontherapeutic research. *Journal of Pediatrics* 149:S25-30.

Mitchell L 1999. Combining focus groups and interviews: Telling how it is; telling how it feels. In *Developing Focus Group Research: Politics, theory and practice*, RS Barbour and J Kitzinger (eds). Sage Publications, London. Pp 36-46.

Morgan David L 1988. *Focus Groups as Qualitative Research*. Sage, Newbury Park.

Morgan DL 1993. *Successful Focus Groups: Advancing the state of the art.* Sage Publications, Newbury Park.

Morgan DL 1997. Planning focus groups. In: *The Focus Group Kit*, DL Morgan & RA Krueger (eds). Sage Publications, Thousand Oaks.

Morgan M, Gibbs S, Maxwell K, Britten N 2002. Hearing children's voices: methodological issues in conducting focus groups with children aged 7-11 years. Qualitative Research 2(1):5-20

Spethman B 1992. Focus groups key to reaching kids. *Advertising Age* 63(6).

Stewart DW and Shamdasani PN 1990. *Focus Groups: Theory and practice*. Sage (Applied Social Research Methods Series), London and Newbury Park.

Trakas DJ 1992. Heavy and light illnesses – and good medicines: Accounts from Greek children. In: *Studying Childhood and Medicine Use*, DJ Trakas and E Sanz (eds). ZHTA Medical Publications, Athens.

Trakas DJ and Sanz EJ (eds) 1992. Studying Childhood and Medicine Use: Perceptions and attitudes. ZHTA Medical Publications, Athens.

Trakas DJ and Sanz EJ (eds) 1996. *Childhood and Medicine Use in Cross-Cultural Perspective.* European Union, Luxembourg.

Winski JM 1992. The ad industry's 'dirty little secret'. *Advertising Age* (June 15): 16.

Wirsing RL and Trakas DJ 1996a. The development of the childhood and medicine use project methodology: The challenges of a multidisciplinary concerted action. In: *Childhood and Medicine Use in Cross-Cultural Perspective,* Trakas DJ and Sanz EJ (eds). European Union, Luxembourg.

Wirsing R and Trakas DJ 1996b. Cross-cultural comparative research: A discourse on using qualitative and quantitative methodologies. In: Children, Medicines and Culture, P Bush, D Trakas, E Sanz, R Wirsing, T Vaskilampi, A Prout (eds). Haworth Press, Binghamton, New York.

Communication and Focus Group Dynamics
An anthropological perspective on children's groups

Michael Anderson

This chapter discusses children's communication in focus groups from the perspective of social anthropology, concentrating on three conceptual frameworks:

- Focus groups as ethnographic events
- Models of children's communication
- Children's communication in groups

Additional ideological and methodological issues which need to be addressed, such as power dynamics and research techniques, will be considered at the relevant points throughout the chapter.

Focus Groups as Ethnographic Events

An ethnographic event could be defined as any live social interaction, bounded by time and space, which the researcher observes and directly or indirectly participates in. The term "ethnographic" implies the interaction of the researcher with the other social actors in the situation, and what is noticed as significant is recorded and becomes part of the process of the "communication of knowledge". Focus groups have all of these dimensions (observation, participation, recording of actions); thus, they might be considered as ethnographic events, at least at this level of description.

The focus group is a research setting in which participants are invited to discuss a topic of importance to – and selected by – the researchers. Using the discussion of the people in the group as "data", researchers facilitate specific discussions and eventually generalize findings on the nature of the topic addressed. In contrast to this pre-defined situation, anthropologists usually research "naturally occurring" social events rather than those which are manufactured or contrived for specific research purposes. They would not normally seek to initiate an event or pre-select the topic as is done with focus groups. Such research tactics would be seen as suspending communication and anthropologists may question the impositions implied in the operating procedures of focus groups.

Social events should be allowed to define themselves, and to begin, unfold, and end, in order for an anthropological analysis to be made. Anthropologists are concerned as much about the intent of the research technique as they are about what is taking place within a natural or contrived context. The focus group needs to be more than a research tool if anthropological knowledge is to be derived from it. Some questions to be considered include: What is the meaning of the focus group for the participants? Should specific characteristics of the children who participate be generalized? Do focus groups generate styles of communicating which would not happen in naturally occurring settings? Only by asking these types of questions and adopting a critical framework which they imply, can focus groups be treated as ethnographic events.

Qualitative research with children

Most writers describing the focus group technique do not discuss the role and involvement of children in the procedure, particularly from the view of the insider (the children). This is not surprising because, aside from laboratory study designs, there has been very little written about children's styles of communication in peer group situations. Qualitative research with children generally remains marginal to that conducted with adults and the relatively few accounts of qualitative research with children, rarely, if ever, adopted a focus group approach (Hurley 1998:2).

Focus groups can be useful in giving children even as young as five years old the space, time and voice to raise issues of importance to them. This is supported by research (Connolly 1995) where the context of the dialogue can create a safe environment for children and set the terms of discussion or activity. Based on her research with 2 ½ to 18 year-old children and youth, Mauthner (1997) emphasizes that negotiations need to be made about consent, privacy and confidentiality. Focus groups are not necessarily empowering for the participants; although the members are permitted the freedom to say what they want, control may be imposed on the children by the adult moderator. As in any other social context, power and control are automatically part of focus group interactions;

e.g., moderators try to keep the group organized and discussion focused, they may control the direction of communication, and children may be interested in intimidating other children or testing the moderator's patience. The exertion of power and control is an issue not only of moderator-to-children communication, but it also appears between children.

Focus group participants, particularly when they are children, can feel intimidated and vulnerable when moderators allow hierarchical relationships to characterize the discussion. Mauthner (1997) argues that a child-centred approach to data collection in groups can assist in dealing with the problem of unequal power relationships in children's focus groups. This implies that children are placed as subjects rather than objects of research and they are treated not only recipients, but also agents and producers of culture and communication. Some of the strategies Mauthner suggests include:

- Allow and encourage children to set their own agenda and talk about their own views.
- Encourage children to describe events through story telling.
- Respect the children's experiences of the research process; e.g. by letting them explore the tape-recording process.

Mauthner also argues for the use of appropriate language styles for children of different ages. Others (Williams et al. 1989) make similar recommendations for aiding communication in group research with children, suggesting that moderators ask children to use their own words rather than expecting them to use and reply with technical or adult terms.

Issues of the anthropological validity of children's focus groups

Focus groups are clearly contrived events, designed with research convenience in mind rather than the flow of naturally occurring social events and processes. However, it should not be assumed that the technique is an invalid research method on these grounds; indeed, anthropologists often hold group discussions with informants during their fieldwork. The important point to remember is that any research setting has limits, not least of which are those imposed by the researcher. Anthropologists would have little difficulty in recognizing the focus group as an ethnographic event provided that all its limitations are acknowledged. For example, it would be erroneous to assume that the interaction and knowledge generated in a focus group is "pure", authentic and natural.

Sink (1991:197) maintains that humans have the tendency to discuss issues and ideas in groups; thus, focus groups might be seen as extensions of naturally formed groups. Whether very young children possess the tendency to engage in group discussion is still debated between developmental psychologists and anthropologists. It has long been established that knowledge is constructed socially (Berger and Luckman 1967) among children as well as adults (James 1993). Sink's observation leans towards a social constructionist model of communication, but does not address the possibility that certain issues can be hidden from group discussions, particularly those in focus group, even with the probing questions of a moderator. What is discussed or explained about personal problems or the family among close friends may be too sensitive to be revealed in the less-familiar group. However, recent research on communication in families has suggested that, for older children, peer groups may be preferable to family groups as a forum for discussing personal concerns (Anderson et al. 2000).

Personal comments, opinions and ideas may be developed according to how people believe others will react (Fishbein and Azjein 1981, Triandis 1980). This is particularly the case when group participants feel compelled or have the tendency to provide answers that they believe will please the moderator or the other participants, rather than address a sensitive personal issue. This is especially a danger when participants are rewarded emotionally or materially for their contributions to the discussion.

Models of Children's Communication

A great deal has been written on the topic of children and communication though rarely, if ever, in the context of discussion groups. The limited research that has been conducted on this topic tends to reflect the bias of psychological models of child development (Prout and James 1990:10). Most of the theorizing and discussion about children and their communicative "competency", until the 1980s, was overwhelmingly concerned with children as "apprentices" for adult life. From this view, children are seen largely for what they will become rather than for what they are; as *becomings* rather than *beings*. Contemporary anthropology re-examines this discourse by proposing that children are active agents in the construction of their own identities. Anthropologists question the idea that children are merely containers to be "filled" with culture by adults, and maintain that the process of social and psychological development is much more dynamic than childhood socialization theory traditionally addressed in the past.

Children and trajectories

The models of children's communication and development which dominate western thought combine biological with social imperatives, wherein communicative elements such as language, gesture and deportment are correlated with physical and psychological maturation. This proposition is in conformity with the idea of "progress" toward adulthood, representing children as moving through different stages on an imaginary trajectory, beginning as incompetent learners with limited social involvement and ending with full social participation – adulthood.

The trajectory model, primarily the accomplishment of Jean Piaget (Ginsberg and Opper 1969) parallels theories of human social evolution wherein young children are seen as pre-social and in need of "cultivation"; i.e., socialization. The standard of "successful" socialization is normally determined by adults according to whether children's psychosocial behaviour is deemed appropriate to their chronological age. For example, by the time children reach the age of five years they are expected to be able to communicate (verbally, emotionally, behaviourally) according to the standards and expectations of their community and culture. Failure to do so may place them in a marginal or socially stigmatized position, in need of special care by parents or outside professionals.

Anthropological theory about childhood challenges the Piagetian model on the grounds that it is a consequence of a specific cultural setting rather than universally valid circumstances. Piaget's legacy continues to dominate research on the development of children's cognition. His paradigm defines a series of stages that children "go through" in order to achieve cognitive and communicative competence. This competence is the mark of adulthood; however, the anthropological perspective suggests that:

> Within such a conceptual scheme children are marginalized beings awaiting temporal passage, through the acquisition of cognitive skill, into the world of adults (Prout and James 1990:11)

This comment draws attention to an underlying assumption of Piaget regarding the "naturalness" and "universality" of childhood, perhaps a reflection of the positivist trends in the 1950s to create a scientific child psychology which could map the progress of all children into adulthood. The "universalized child", the image produced by research about children during this era, was visualized as a creature that progresses through a series of biological, cognitive and communicative phases, which attest to her/his successful "development". The steps in the process are visualized as natural and invariant "phases" which decrease irrationality and incompetence, independent of what "rational" and "competence" mean in different sociocultural contexts. Indeed the cliché, often expressed by parents in western cultures, "It's just a phase she's going through" is a reminder of the how the Piagetian model is reflected in everyday life (Prout and James 1990:12).

Anthropological perspectives on childhood

Anthropological perspectives and theory take issue with the validity of the naturalness and the universality of childhood. The discipline of anthropology includes a long history of research about cross-cultural childhood socialization (Mead 1928, Whiting and Child 1953) and, more recently about children's communication with each other (Briggs 1970, Bluebond-Langer 1978). These processes involve complex communicative dynamics which anthropologists have attempted to elucidate and interpret from their research with children, arguing that it is inappropriate to view childhood as simply a phase of development toward adulthood. Children are agents in the construction of their own communicative competencies as well as of others, including adults and particularly their parents.

Ochs (1988) supports a model of communication development which accounts for the impact that adults have on children and also addresses the impact that children have on adults. To this model could be added the influence children have on each other because of the presence of an adult, and the impact adults have on each other because of the presence or involvement of children. Ochs' point is that when adults and children encounter each other in communicative contexts, both are affected and transformed in their thoughts, feelings and behaviours, and therefore in their communicative modes. Gaskins and Lucy (1987) also maintain that when adults routinely interact with children they are forced to adapt in ways which affect their own cultural practices. Thus, children are clearly producers of communication for others as well as acquirers of communication skills for themselves.

The dynamics of interactive situations, such as those produced in focus groups, provide a rich data source for observers of communication and present challenging problems for analysis and interpretation. For example, how is sense to be made of how children communicate in the specific and highly contrived context of the focus group? Children's perceptions of time, space and what is expected of them in group interactions provide coherence. Focus group moderators recognize that these static concepts are not usually realized in group discussions, and that dynamism, fluidity and individual interpretations require sensitivity to subtle meanings for particular children in particular contexts.

Children's Communication in Groups

> *Pooh began to feel a little more comfortable, because when you are a bear of Very Little Brain, and think of Things, you find that a Think which seemed very thingish inside of you is quite different when it gets out into the open and has other people looking at it. (AA Milne 1929)*

What seems "thingish" (plausible, self-evident, obvious, not requiring words) in our minds before we discuss it can look quite different after we have discussed it with others. We can all recall from personal experience how an experience, idea, or thought that seems quite clear and distinct can become far less clear and distinct when it is discussed and shared with others. Alternatively, what may seem vague and quite imprecise can be clarified when discussed. Either way, the "thingishness" is changed when it is discussed. People's unwillingness for ideas, thoughts and/or feelings to be changed may explain their hesitation to discuss them. Indeed, it can be risky to talk about things with others who may not understand and who may not realise how sensitive the issue is. Engaging others in discussion is a calculated risk; gains and losses are weighed before and during the process. As Goffman (1975) emphasizes, there is a "strategic" aspect of social interaction, with potential advantages to be gained and potential losses to be conceded. Thus, even under the best of conditions, much of human interaction is a risky enterprise for children as well as for adults.

Children learn from other children as well as from the adults with whom they interact what can be gained and lost through simply communicating with each other. Opie and Opie (1977) describe the importance that young children place on maintaining the rules of a game. James (1993) emphasizes that young children want to appear the same as others in their age cohort, while older children want to be seen as slightly different from their peers.

Anthropologists are attuned to a number of important issues with respect to children's focus groups and which constitute the dynamics underlying the visible aspects of the culture of the event; among these are pretence, conformity and compliance, and silence. These dimensions are not exclusive to focus group but apply to any participatory experience or ethnographic interview.

Pretence

> *The first person he met was Rabbit.*
> *"Hallo Rabbit", said Pooh, "is that you?"*
> *"Let's pretend it isn't" said Rabbit, "and see what happens."*
> *(AA Milne 1926)*

Goldman (1998:1) uses this excerpt from Milne's stories about Winnie the Pooh to provide a literary rendition of a common conversational practice of children. The players in its fiction are projected as "child-like"; they undertake changes of identity in a game of pretend. He reflects on the excerpt by relating it to how children interact with each other and with adults, and most crucially to doing research with them. Importantly, the ability to make sense of this passage is, like that of the characters themselves, dependent on shared knowledge about make-believe routines, role playing, and the kinds of social information these representations incorporate. According to Goldman, the issue of children's acting out of pretence as precisely the quality which contributes to their being children. Although his examples are drawn from a specific ethnographic context (the Huli people of Papua, New Guinea) and far removed from that of a focus group discussion conducted in Europe, they are applicable to children in many settings. This is corroborated by the work of Bluebond-Langer (1978), James (1993) and Anderson (1996).

Pretence is often a part of how children experiment with and control their own social worlds, and their feelings and the feelings of others. When children discuss their personal experiences, they play with pretence – as do adults. It would, however, be crass and inaccurate to suggest that they purposely lie; pretence is simply a part of children's experimentation with social control. Moreover, in the context of a discussion between children, it is possible that once experiences and feelings have been verbally expressed, they readily become parts of and embellishments of other children's narratives, which in turn reshape their own stories and feelings.

In short, the sharing of thoughts and feelings is a high-risk strategy for focus group participants, especially when they are children. It is risky for the participants because, being children and particularly sensitive to the reactions of others to them, anything they say could result in their appearing too different from their peers (see James 1993). The personal agenda of children is likely to be more important to them than the research agenda of the moderator. Asking children to share feelings and experiences is also risky for moderators, precisely because of the dynamics of pretence. The moderator's appreciation of these dynamics can mean the difference between eliciting honest and open responses or getting highly ambiguous, muted or non-responses.

The process of how feelings, ideas and thoughts develop is more akin to what is referred to in sociology and anthropology as social constructionism than pretence. It can easily become pretence when children are not entirely honest about their feelings and experiences, or portray themselves as the same as others so as not to feel different. This tendency is not unique to children, but unless a moderator is aware of the dynamics of pretence, an entire fiction can be woven into the group interactions.

It is not only children who engage in pretence during focus groups. The adult moderators might also be drawn into the theatre, and their pretence lies in the performance they must achieve by being understanding of and understandable to children in order to create the feeling (or at least the illusion) that they comprehend the children's experiences. Moreover, the adoption of words and actions deemed by the moderator to be sufficiently "child-like" to encourage the participants in the group to share opinions and experience is also pretence, but deemed necessary to the "success" of the exercise. The moderators of children's focus groups try to develop a child-centred context by playing a role that they would not normally play. This is a form of pretence, much the same as the reply of Rabbit when asked if he is an adult … "Let's pretend I'm not and see what happens".

Conformity and compliance

Referring to her fieldwork in primary schools, Allison James (1993) recalls a conversation between two 6 year-olds discussing the contents of their sandwiches which they brought from their homes.

> What have you got in your sandwiches?
> Corned beef.
> I've got corned beef as well.
> We've got the same.
> I've got a biscuit - a club.
> I had one of those yesterday.
> I had the same as you yesterday and today.
> (laughter…)

The celebratory laughter at the end of this excerpt stems from the recognized coincidental "sameness" the children share. The example is used by James to illustrate the value that children of this age place on identifying with each other and on appearing the same as their peers. Even saying the "right thing" in the "right way" can be of importance to children in terms of the social dynamics within their age group. Their concerns about this can easily override the importance of giving truthful responses to the questions of the researcher. For children, it is essential to maintain pleasant relations with their peers; perhaps more important than pleasing the moderator.

According to Albrecht et al. (1993:55), "identification" is the tendency for people to want to be the same as their co-participants in a group. By saying the same thing as their peers, children identify with their friends rather than appearing different from them. In the group they may follow the example of another participant whose opinion they think is important or whom they admire. Some children, out of shyness, embarrassment, or genuine unawareness about what is being discussed, may not say anything; remaining quiet may influence other children to do the same.

Even though children are capable of dismissing the comments and opinions of adults, moderators can provoke deference from children in focus groups. Because the moderator is an unknown quantity children may say what they think the moderator wants to hear, at least initially. Thus moderators need to direct their attention towards how and on what topic the children engage in the discussion. Pleasing the moderator for some children may be akin to pleasing their teacher, and moderators need to be careful about what they say and how they respond to children's opinions. An overly enthusiastic response to a comment from one child, accompanied by cool reception to an opposing view expressed by another could sway the discussion in the direction of the former. As a result, an apparent but false consensus is reached, or friction is developed between the child expressing the dissenting view and the other children - or the moderator.

The research of James (1986) shows that the effort of children to be the same as their peers becomes modified as they approach adolescence. They no longer want to be like all of their peers but want to be slightly different, either as individuals or as members of a select group. Pre-adolescents and young teenagers, in an effort to establish some measure of their own uniqueness, try to avoid being one among many in a big crowd, and become more selective in developing and expressing their individual image. While focus groups with young children often result in consensus between the children and compliance with the moderator, those with pre-adolescents can reveal discord. The authority of the adult moderator is challenged, children select other children with whom they think alliances can be formed, and children who are perceived as not being "in" by their peers are excluded.

Techniques can be developed to minimize scenarios of pretence and compliance that occur in research with groups. For example, participants could be asked to respond to questions in writing and read to the group by the moderator without identifying the author to generate discussion (Van de Ven and Delbecq 1971). This approach "randomizes" group interaction and may help to impede the possibility of compliance, pretence, and so forth; however it depersonalizes the interaction. Children are not likely to be enthusiastic about writing down their answers and listening to a series of anonymous responses. They may interpret the situation as a "test", and become visibly agitated (either negatively or positively) when they hear their answer read -- negating the intended anonymity of the technique.

Silence

It is quite common for focus group participants to be hesitant to speak, inattentive or distracted (Krueger 1997:61). The reason for their lack of involvement requires investigation and understanding by the moderator. The silence of one or all of the participants should neither be interpreted as agreement with comments, nor taken as evidence that they disagree. Silence is ambiguous and it forms the unspoken text in data analysis.

A focus group can reach a point where the moderator thinks it is ended simply because there is silence. As with any other qualitative research methodology, focus groups require skill in organization and maintenance to make and keep them viable. There is more to group techniques than simply "keeping a conversation going" for its own sake. Silence is not usually isolated, it is contextual. Silence among children (as for adults) is silence for a reason, perhaps related to the topic, the mood of particular participants, or the manner of a moderator. It is for the moderator to make a decision about what the silence means – the termination of a discussion or simply a pause. Silence can also reveal a great deal about what children will or not discuss and under what circumstances.

Other Anthropological Concerns

This overview of children's focus groups from an anthropological viewpoint highlights some aspects that could be useful in planning and conducting the discussions, and in the analysis of the material generated by the process. It should not be assumed that children's focus groups held in one cultural setting will be identical in form and content to those conducted in another. There are always discernible individual, cultural and socio-economic variations in experience, expectations, behaviour, and knowledge. All of these differences can be reviewed from the perspective of relationships between children, adults and children, health professionals and children, health professionals and parents, and other dimensions relevant to the cultural setting.

The above observation raises the issue, particularly in the comparative discipline of anthropology, of what should be compared when focus groups take place in different cultural contexts. Is "like being compared with like", or does the focus group process intrinsically differ from culture to culture? Are the understandings of what constitutes a focus group the same for all concerned, or is the comparison merely about interactions between the participants in different cultures? For the anthropologist, communication in all of its forms, including in a focus group, provides a tool to comprehend individual as well as cultural meanings. Opinions expressed, stories related, and feelings alluded to are not merely isolated individual attitudes; they also constitute historical, social, contemporary indications of personal identity in a specific social context in a particular cultural setting. Ambiguity and ambivalence, along with inconsistency and contradiction are grist for the communication mill. They force qualitative researchers to rehumanize the study of communication and direct it toward the respect of individuality rather than the homogenizing of the category "childhood".

References

Albrecht TL, Johnson GM, Walther JB 1993. Understanding communication processes in focus groups. In: *Successful Focus Groups: Advancing the state of the art* (A Sage Focus Edition), DL Morgan (ed). Sage, London.

Anderson M 1996. *Childhood, Culture and Identity*, Unpublished Ph.D Thesis, University of Hull.

Anderson M, Tunaley J and Walker J 2000. *Relatively Speaking: Communication in the family*. British Telecommunications Forum, London.

Berger P and Luckman T 1967. *The Social Construction of Reality: A treatise in the sociology of knowledge*. Penguin, Harmondsworth.

Bluebond-Langer M 1978. *The Private Worlds of Dying Children*. Princeton University Press, Princeton, New Jersey.

Briggs CL 1986. *Learning How to Ask: A sociolinguistic appraisal of the role of the interview*. Cambridge University Press, Cambridge, UK.

Connolly P 1995. *An Interdisciplinary Conference on Children and Social Competence*. University of Surrey, UK.

Fishbein M and Azjein I 1981. Acceptance, yielding, and impact: Cognitive processes in persuasion. In: *Cognitive Responses in Persuasion*, RE Petty, TM Ostrom and TM Brock (eds). Lawrence Erlbaum, Hillsdale, New Jersey.

Gaskins S and Lucy JA 1987. The role of children in the production of adult culture: A Yucatec case. Paper Presented at the Annual Meeting of the American Ethnological Society, Held Jointly with the Society for Psychological Anthropology, New Orleans.

Ginsburg H and Opper SS (eds) 1969, *Piaget's Theory of Intellectual Development: An introduction*. Englwood Cliffs, New Jersey.

Goffman E 1982 [1967]. *Interaction Ritual: Essays on face-to-face behaviour*. Pantheon Books, New York.

Goldman LR 1988. *Child's Play: Myth, mimesis and make-believe*. Berg, New York.

Goodnow JJ 1990. The socialisation of cognition: What is involved? In: *Cultural Psychology: Essays on comparative human development*, JW Stigler, RA Schweder, and G Herdt (eds). Cambridge University Press, Cambridge, UK.

Hurley N 1998. *Straight Talk: Working With children and young people in groups*. Joseph Rowntree Foundation, York, UK.

James A 1986. Learning to belong: The boundaries of adolescence. In: *Symbolising Boundaries: Identity and diversity in British cultures*, AP Cohen (ed). Manchester University Press, Manchester, UK.

James A 1993. *Childhood Identities: Self and social relationships in the life of the child*. Edinburgh University Press, Edinburgh.

Krueger RA 1997. *Moderating Focus Group* (Focus Group Kit). Sage, London.

Krueger RA 1998. *Involving Community Members in Focus Groups* (Focus Group Kit). Sage, London.

Mauthner M 1997. Methodological aspects of collecting data from children: Lessons from three research projects. *Children and Society* 11:16-28.

Mead M 1928. *Coming of Age in Samoa.* Morrow, New York.

Morgan DL 1988. *The Focus Group Guidebook.* Sage, London.

Ochs E 1988. *Culture and Language Development: Language acquisition and language socialisation in a Samoan Village.* Cambridge University Press, Cambridge.

Opie L and Opie P 1977. *The Lore and Language of Schoolchildren.* Paladin, London.

Prout A and James A 1990. A new paradigm for the sociology of childhood? In: *Constructing and Reconstructing Childhood,* A James and A Prout (eds). Falmer Press, London.

Sink DW 1991. Focus groups as an approach to outcome assessment. *American Review of Public Administration* 21: 97-204.

Triandis HC 1980. Values, attitudes, and interpersonal behavior. In: *Nebraska Symposium on Motivation* (Vol. 27), HE How (ed). University of Nebraska Press, Lincoln, Nebraska.

Van de Ven AH and Delbecq AL 1971. Nominal vs interacting group processes for committee decision making effectiveness. *Academy of Management Journal* 14:203-212.

Whiting JWM and Child IL 1953. *Child Training and Personality: A cross-cultural study.* Yale University Press, New Haven, Connecticut.

Williams T et al. 1989. *A Way In: Five key areas of health education.* HEA, London.

What Moderators Need to Know
Children's developmental characteristics and focus groups

Maria Vega and Pilar Aramburuzabala

What do moderators need to know about 7 to 12 year-old children that can help them to conduct focus groups effectively with this age cohort? The experience gained from the *Living with Asthma in Childhood* project substantiates that the focus group technique can be used productively with young children. However, it requires some child-centred modifications and a clear understanding on the part of the researchers of how the focus group context is interpreted by children. Being aware of what children think, feel and want is a central issue which should be addressed by all group moderators who wish to satisfy children's educational and social needs. How children behave and what they say does not necessarily coincide with what they feel, think, or know. This phenomenon is not exclusive to children; it accompanies human beings throughout their lives.

This chapter addresses four concepts that will help moderators to understand 7 to 12 year-old children's behaviour while participating in a focus group:

- Operatory intelligence
- Mental modes
- Knowledge and problem solving
- Interaction and auto-reflexivity

The constructivist perspective used in this chapter is from the work of several scientists such as Piaget, Vygotsky, Bruner and Wertsch who maintain that human cognitive development is the result of learning that takes place during the interaction between individuals and their social environment. The socio-cognitive model is based on the idea that knowledge is constructed by the learner who assigns meaning and makes experiences significant according to her/his way of thinking, feeling and acting. According to this paradigm, the process of thinking is a function of trials with problem solving and development is measured by the individual's progress in problem solving within her/his sociocultural context. Consequently, knowledge originates within a specific context and is significant only within that location.

The constructivist socio-cognitive model defines cognition and thinking as problem-solving. In focus groups, children are confronted with solving a problem about a topic selected by the researcher, with the intent of using their flexible capacity of improvisation. The children are expected to participate in the discussion in the most spontaneous way possible, in spite of the fact that they are acting in an intentionally planned or contrived situation. Cognitive processes guide the action in an intelligent, interpersonal and practical way towards a goal – or expectation. The goals that children aim for imply the presence of other persons, and they have feelings attached. Thinking, feeling and acting intervene in an integral manner when children are confronted with reaching a goal or expectation; i.e., solving a problem.

The expectations of a 7 year-old child who participates in a focus group can be very different from those of 12 year-old. Moreover the goals of the researchers and moderators are not the same as the expectations of the children in the focus group. Understanding the purposes of the children when they participate in a focus group will help to explain their behaviour.

Operatory Intelligence

For Piaget (1932), the primary goal of cognitive development is the acquisition of skill in mental operations. According to his developmental scales, children of 7 to 12 years of age are in the period of concrete operations. At all levels of development, knowledge is defined as the consequence of the person's action when he/she acts with his/her environment. Actions which are internalized by the subject in a reversible way and integrated into his/her knowledge structure are referred to as "operations".

According to Piaget, 7 to 12 year-old children are able to use logical operations as a cognitive tool. It is important for focus group moderators to realize that the major limitation of this period is that children need to process "concrete" information; that is, optically perceptible information. When faced with a task, children think about the elements exactly as they visually appear. It is difficult for them to imagine, to make projections or to take into account possible theoretical and abstract situations; in the event that they do, it will always be as an extension of reality. As children mature, they develop the ability to separate themselves from visible and observable reality, enabling them to concentrate on problem resolution, taking into account all possible situations and causal relationships. If, at the beginning of this stage, “the possible” is subordinated to “the real”, little by little the child will subordinate “the real” to “the possible”.

More recent research has added to Piaget’s findings showing that what places children at a higher maturity level in terms of their ways of confronting problems is not primarily their chronological age, but rather their educational experiences and their knowledge of the subject of the task which must be completed or the problem that has to solved. In focus groups, children face at least two challenges: 1) To participate and interact in a group which addresses a topic chosen and put forth by the moderator, and 2) to develop communicative exchanges with others about that topic. Not all children come into the situation with the same knowledge and this will condition their individual ways of operating. Some will need extra support in order to understand what they are doing and talking about, while others will easily handle the situation by thinking and speaking about the topic, all the while using their ability to think abstractly.

Mental Modes

Donaldson’s (1996) findings support Piaget’s propositions about mental development and defend the concept of different modes which help to explain the way the human mind works. These modes appear as the individual develops and they are not mutually exclusive. They never disappear and each mode evolves over time. Each mode is defined by two criteria: 1) the locus of concern and 2) the way in which distinct components of experience (emotions, perceptions, feelings) relate to each other. In this model, the locus of concern is defined in a temporal sense; e.g., what a person feels and perceives at any specific time -- and, as a consequence, how the person behaves.

For very young children, the locus of concern is always the present moment, the "here-and-now"; this is the precise mode. Gradually, due to life experiences and expanding capabilities, children develop a new locus of concern which includes their personal past and future; the linear mode. When operating in the linear mode, people are able to take a look back at what they have experienced and what has happened in their lives, but they are also capable of looking ahead, towards possible future events. The precise and linear modes constitute the framework of real and specific events.

According to Donaldson, the linear mode is followed by the impersonal mode in which the mind allows people to reach a degree of independence from personal goals because they are able to consider problems as generalities. In the impersonal mode, the locus of concern shifts away from specific people and events, and thoughts and emotions are separated from individualistic, egocentric views. Compared to the linear mode where personal problems are managed by attempts to make or prevent events from happening, the impersonal mode is characterized by a more global understanding of situations. Personal problems are no longer viewed as simply cause-and-effect; instead they are treated as part of a larger whole. Problem-solving is a result of a shift in the locus of concern; and in the impersonal mode problems are often solved without the person being aware of the actual component which led to the solution.

Focus group moderators need to be aware of these modes and appreciate that children can think and act according to different modes. Seven to 12 year-old children are likely to be function somewhere between the linear and the impersonal mode; however it would not be unusual if some are operating primarily in the precise, here-and-now, precise mode. As with other developmental stages, differences are more related to maturity than to chronological age.

Some examples from the *Living with Asthma in Childhood* project might illuminate the locus of concern model. When asked about sports and possible limitations of activities due to asthma, the children's comments could be classified according to categories which define the various mental modes. Some children based their comments on concrete realities, using the precise mode; e.g., they spoke about precise experiences while playing specific games. Others established cause-effect relationships characteristic of the linear mode; for example, "If you smoke, you can't play sports well", or, "If you are fat, you have problems with sports". Other children made generalizations in the impersonal mode, such as referring to the idea of "limitations" due to asthma.

Knowledge and Problem Solving

Focus group discussions make it possible to learn about children's knowledge because the members of the group are challenged with a problem-solving situation. Because the focus group is a planned event, the children know that something is expected from them and sense that they are required to act and respond according to a protocol which may or may not be clear to them at the beginning. The task they are presented with, that of discussing a specific topic necessitates their full concentration and attention, just as with any other learning activity.

This involvement obliges that children draw upon affective components such as attitudes and values, as well as cognitive components, specifically paying attention, listening, selecting and establishing relationships, and being conscious about these processes. The components which the children put to work and their integration of them will depend on the meaning that they assign to the task as well as on the cognitive and affective tools they have at their disposal.

It may be noted that adults in focus groups function in much the same way as described above; however, there is one big difference. Adults can refuse to attend a focus group if, for example, their feel that their participation will not have meaning for them. Children do not have this option: They may not be able to predict if the event will be a meaningful (or enjoyable, fun or entertaining), and parents make the final decision about their child's participation (hopefully, after taking their child's opinion into consideration). Adults can also withdraw their participation during a focus group if they evaluate that taking part does not suit them. Children, on the other hand, may continue to participate due to peer pressure or the desire to please the moderator – even after the group interaction ceases to be fun or interesting.

In order to make focus group tasks meaningful for children, moderators need to keep some principles in mind. First, children should have a clear understanding of the objectives and the conditions under which the session will take place. Moderators must help children understand what is expected of them by adjusting their description to the cognitive capacities of the participants in each group. They also must take into account affective factors so that the children perceive the task as attractive, or at least meeting a need. Moderators must not only motivate the children to stay with the group, but they also have to maintain the children's interest. They need to help all the children feel that they are capable of participating in the task, that their contribution is important, and that the task is completed in an interesting and pleasant manner.

Secondly, children need to feel the sense of a challenge, but a challenge that is within their capabilities, even though it may require a considerable effort and may appear strange or difficult at the beginning. The tasks of the focus group should have an "intermediate" difficulty; even though it is a new experience, it should be an activity which is based on supportive cognitive and affective skills which children have developed from previous experiences. Some children will feel incapable of performing the tasks (e.g., interacting) when they perceive that other children in the group have a greater capacity for taking into account and handling opinions from the rest of the participants. As a result, they may passively tolerate the experience or, develop negative feelings or behaviours.

Children's perceptions and expectations of the focus group context need to be anticipated by the moderators. Some children are able to concentrate on the topic under discussion; others lose focus and "wander". The unfamiliar context of a focus group may lead some children to be timid; others to become aggressive (e.g., making fun of others in the group); and others to play the role of the group clown, continually interrupting in order to gain attention. When these apprehensive or disruptive behaviours appear, moderators need to work within the context of the group dynamics and find appropriate ways to "neutralize" them. The paramount role of the moderator is to help all the children feel secure during the session and carry good feelings with them about the experience after it ends.

Moderators should be prepared to adjust their speech to the children's specific characteristics. For example, children's answers to previous questions will indicate the form in which topics can be presented. In our focus groups, we managed the questions differently according to the age of the children; for example, in groups of 11 and 12 year-olds, the children were asked if they felt that asthma placed limitations on them. In contrast, for 7 year-olds, the same topic needed to be more concrete; for example, "Can children with asthma play ball or compete in swimming meets?"

In focus groups where the age range of the children is mixed (i.e., several ages from 7 to 12 years are represented), moderators need to use a variety of questioning strategies. Direct questions may produce answers but interfere with promoting interaction, as the short and truncated answers as the example below illustrates.

Moderator: What did you think about the video?
Andreas (12 years old): Whose turn is it?
Moderator: Anybody's.
Andreas: It was nice.
Moderator: Tell us, Andreas.
Andreas: It showed us how we can deal with asthma and which medicines we must take.
George (10 years old): And what causes asthma?
Moderator: And what causes asthma?
George: Dust.
Anastasia (8 years old): Plants.

Moderator: What else?
Andreas: Animals.
Anastasia: Pollen.

In contrast, when more flexible questions are used, children of different ages can be drawn into conversation with each other as demonstrated by the following rich interchange between 8 and 12 year-olds.

Moderator: How do you feel when you take your medicines in the presence of other children? Or does this never happen with you?
Anne (8 year-old): It rarely happens that my friends are present during intake. Because I have to take it in the mornings and evenings. Only sometimes my friends stay longer with me (in the house).
Eric (12 year-old): My friends got used to it. They know it, they even remind me sometimes that I should take it. Before they used to ask, "What is this? What are you taking there?" And whether I always take it and so on. I explained them.
Doreen (12 year-old): All the children in my class know that I have asthma and thus they never say anything when I take my medicines.
Jens (12 year-old): My friend also has asthma. Once he had an asthma attack, and since he had forgotten is spray, I gave him mine.

Interaction and Auto-Reflexivity

Applying a focus group structure developed for adults to children's groups means that children need to become capable of participating in and mastering tasks with which they may not be familiar. For example, they need to learn how to give and listen to opinions, to respect the others' turn to speak, and to remain quiet when others are talking. According to developmental theory, children evolve from subjective and egocentric attitudes to auto-reflexive ones. The chronological age when the auto-reflexive stage appears varies according to individual differences which are the result of a dialectic interaction between children and their life experiences from the environment.

Most seven year-old children are able to participate in a focus group discussion because they can recognize that others have personal perspectives which are subjective. Even though they are still in the egocentric stage, they are capable of accepting that the "other" may see things differently from the way they do. According to Piaget, egocentrism – a lack of ability for taking into consideration the point of view of another person – is characteristic of pre-operatory thinking.

Children in this stage have difficulty in coordinating different points of view. They tend to identify with their parents' point of view because they recognize that their parents' intention to take care them and concern for their well-being. They see parents as "right" because they "know" more than their children do. They accept that parents may punish them or forbid them from doing certain things because they realize that parents protect them from harm and "teach" them to grow up.

As children mature and gain more experience, they move away from the subjective, ego-centred attitude and become auto-reflexive (Selman 1976). They become capable of integrating their own perspectives with those of others such as parents and peers. However, in this stage, they are still not able to integrate the perspectives of an impartial third party; for example those of a teacher, and most certainly those of a group moderator. In moving towards the auto-reflexive stage, children become aware that other people will argue on behalf of their own perspectives; thus, children begin to recognize that there may be reciprocal influences between their own beliefs and those of others. They are capable of realizing that their parents, whom they acknowledge as their advisors and guides, may feel pleasure in seeing them growing up and being happy. They also discover that their parents are not always right and they also recognize that parents may even disagree with unconditional obedience (Piaget 1932).

Sometimes parents succeed in changing their children's behaviour, but with no guarantee that they have made a change in their attitudes. Changes in children's attitudes and behaviours are also a result of interaction with their peers; interacting with equals helps them to modify attitudes and behaviours. Children's focus group place young people in a situation where they have a chance to interact with their peers, their equals.

Auto-reflexivity and learning

The participation of children in an adult-moderated focus group extends the mode of behaviour which they have learned to use with parents, teachers, and other adult authority figures. For example, when children first attend day care centres or primary school they tend to develop an intense affective relationship with the teacher, similar to the feelings that they have for their parents. Children's feelings of dependence and trust in their parents lead them to accept unconditionally the authority of both parents and teachers. This acceptance has implications for the way that children participate in focus groups. The moderator, by virtue of being an adult, might represent the unquestionable authority of parent / teacher to children.

Focus groups give children the opportunity to question themselves, which leads to inner conflict and a disruption of their cognitive balance. As children advance in their psychosocial development, they begin to question adult authority. They also begin to recognize discrepancies between what they themselves say and what they do, and between what other children say and do. Intersubjective and intrasubjective conflicts might result; i.e., respectively, cognitive conflict caused by interaction with others and internal cognitive imbalance. These new insights may bring children into conflict with others (parents, teachers, other children) but also give rise to internal conflicts.

When these conflicts are within the limits of what children are capable of resolving, a change in their thinking may result and new learning may take place. Young children see parents as authority figures, but also see them as the source of love, care and protection; they transfer this view to their teachers. Later, they see parents as adults who send conflicting signals, or they observe that their friends' parents behave differently with their children from the way their own parents treat them. They absorb these "data" and begin to understand that adults are not always necessary "right". Depending on children's developmental level and their ability to sort things out, they might behave in the focus group as "good little soldiers" or, alternatively resent or confront the "foreign" moderator for intruding in their life and asking questions.

Practical implications for moderators

For some children, depending on their social-affective development, their relationship with the moderator will be easier than for others. Moderators need to be aware of children's attitudes about adults as authority figures, caregivers and protectors, and be prepared to implement creative ways of interacting with the children within this framework. For example, children who are intimidated by the talents and competencies of other children may see the moderator as a protector. Moderators should present themselves as people who bring the children together to have a good time, not to be tested, in the hope that experiences will be freely shared, without the need for adult approval. They need to emphasize that they want to learn from the children and that the reason they are present is to listen and learn – not to correct.

During the first few moments of the session moderators need to create the feeling that what children say is essential, and that the views and experiences of all the children are of equal importance. As an outcome of the interaction with equals, children will be able to construct and express their ideas by making them explicit in a non-threatening atmosphere.

As a final note, the meanings that children assign to their knowledge and experiences are related to their immediate context, particularly their family setting. Obtaining and comparing the feedback of the children with that of the parents can become an important source of information in research in education and health policy. Therefore, whenever focus groups with children are conducted, researchers should also consider the possibility of organizing parallel groups with the parents.

References

Donaldson M 1996. *Una Exploración de la Mente Humana* [trans *Human Minds: An Exploration*]. Morata, Madrid.

Novak JD 1998. *Learning, Creating, and Using Knowledge. Concept maps as facilitative tools in schools and corporations*. Lawrence Erlbaun Associates, Hillsdale, New Jersey.

Piaget J 1932. *Le Jugement Moral chez l'Enfant.* Presses Universitaires de France, Paris.

Selman RT 1976. Social cognitive understanding: A guide to educational and clinical practice. In: *Moral Development and Behavior*, T Lickona (ed). Holt, New York.

Training Focus Group Moderators
An exploratory and experimental model

Annette Drews

The task of the focus group moderator during the discussion session is to facilitate communication between the participants. In the prototype focus group, as detailed in many handbooks for using the technique with adults, it is recommended that two researchers share the duties. One acts as the active moderator by explaining the subject, making introductions, posing questions, inviting the participants to interact, and helping to keep the discussion focused. The second moderator acts primarily in an observational role, keeping notes which help to identify each speaker on the audio recording and making notations about non-verbal behaviour. The responsibilities of both moderators continue after the session has been completed. They review the audio recording, compare notes and impressions, and prepare for the analysis of the content of the session. This model has become standard for adult focus groups, and with good training of adult moderators to speak with and observe other adults, the system usually functions quite well.

For focus groups with children, in view of the obvious age difference between the moderators and participants, moderator training takes on a new dimension and requires the consideration of factors which are often taken for granted in adult groups. This chapter presents the author's experiences with organizing a training course for moderators of focus groups with 7 to 11 year-old children, in collaboration with the *Living with Asthma in Childhood* project. Since there is very little bibliography which systematically addresses the issue of training moderators for children's groups in detail, this article is intended to be an experimental guide. It reviews the training course, based on the author's background in anthropology and psychology, and includes the rationale for the training materials used. It is hoped that the approach will be used and modified by others involved in the training of moderators for children's focus group discussions.

The Context of the Training Course

Eight third-year university students from the Fachbereich Sozialwesen (Faculty of Social Sciences), Hochschule Zittau/Goerlitz, were selected to attend the training course. The size of the group was based on considerations related to the target number of groups to be conducted as well as to logistics of interaction. In larger groups, bonds of friendship and sharing are difficult to establish. The concept of a training course requires a psychologically safe atmosphere which allows the participants to open up to each other so that they can learn the necessary communication skills.

During a period of six months, 4-hour training sessions were held once a week in the therapy room of the university, a spacious but cosy environment. The carpeting in the room allowed for sitting in informal ways and even stretching out and lying down on the floor for guided relaxation in order to facilitate processes of personal interaction. The room was equipped with a television, video and CD-player as well as other types of material useful for creative expression important in group moderation. These resources were used to great benefit during both the theoretical part of the training sessions and the implementation of the focus groups which were conducted towards the end of the course.

Theoretical Principles

In order to predict the kind of skills and knowledge required to conduct effective focus groups with children, it is necessary to answer the following questions:

- ♦ Are focus groups with young children different from (or the same as) those with adults or with adolescents?
- ♦ Should they be expected to be different and why?
- ♦ In what ways are focus groups with children similar to those with adults?

Focus groups with children are expected to be different from those with adults because these two age groups are in different life-cycle phases which influence emotional, social and intellectual modes of response (see for example, Bornstein and Lamb 1992, Keller 1998). The emotional and social aspects of a given situation bear more importance for children than for adults.

- ♦ Emotionally, children have fewer defence mechanisms than adults and react to situations in terms of their needs for security and acceptance. In contrast, adult emotions are influenced by needs for social belonging, status and prestige as well as consciously formulated personal goals.

- ♦ Socially, children are less prejudiced than adults and more open to social, religious and ethnic group variation. Intellectually, children are more curious and learn faster than adults, but have limited background reference points. As a result, children are less able than adults to define a situation with respect to its intellectual purpose.

The general points outlined above mean that the focus group experience is different for children, and it is essential that their emotional, social and intellectual capacities are considered when introducing the session to them. Apart from the practical aspects of setting up the group activity with children, the moderators also must be prepared in a special way to meet the children's needs, a point which will be addressed later in this article.

When issues of age differences are set aside, focus groups either with children or adults share some similarities. They have the same objective of generating ideas or stimulating a rich level of participants' reflections about a specific topic (Debus 1995:30). The dynamics of the group should help to stimulate the participant's expression of attitudes and knowledge, and to increase their validity. Children's and adult focus groups share many practical considerations, and one of these is the training of moderators. The moderators of children's groups need to be trained in two complementary areas: 1) moderation theory and practical skills, and 2) specific techniques in facilitating interaction in groups of children.

Moderation Theory and Practical Skills

The course included a review of the vast amount of literature about moderation theory and communication techniques (see for example, Thoman, Schultz and von Thun 1988, Doppler and Lautenburg 1995). One of the central ideas emphasized was the continuum of human experience including sensual, physiological, mental, social and intellectual processes. These are all relevant to the focus group interaction because they influence the perception and the creation of the group by each and every participant, including the moderators.

Based on the assumption that learning about the life experience involves a continuum, it was necessary to minimize purely rational ways of knowledge transfer as much as possible in lectures and discussions. In order to achieve this, use was made of the extremely entertaining collection of interactive games and exercises described by Maaß and Ritschl (1997) in their book with the telling title *Teamgeist* (teamspirit). These games and exercises enabled the students to learn the skills of effective moderation by doing, acting, and acting-out.

At the practical level, according to Mary Debus (1995:36) good moderators are people who:

- Feel at ease and comfortable with other people; hence they are relaxed and not threatened by personal interaction with others.

- Have the ability to put others at ease, with the result that others naturally open up to them quickly.

- Project unconditional regard and acceptance of others, and are genuinely (or can appear to be) non-judgemental.

- Convey warmth and empathy, projecting understanding of the feelings and thoughts of others.

- Possess good verbal and interpersonal skills; hence they interact well in many different situations with a variety of types of people, and can use language in such a way as to seem like one of the group.

- Have good listening skills, paying close attention to what others say, and do not feel compelled to inject their own thoughts and comments into the conversation.

- Project enthusiasm, are genuinely interested in others and whose own enthusiasm stimulates heightened interest from others.

- Are aware of the power of non-verbal reactions and are capable of controlling their own body language and facial expressions to project the traits described above and not convey annoyance or frustration.

- Are able to conceptualize and to think through contingencies, as opposed to thinking literally and in a rote manner.

Some people "simply have the right combination of personal traits and raw talent to make effective moderators" (Debus 1995:37). Is it possible find "saints" like these to moderate focus groups, particularly for children's groups? Assuming that the above pleasant traits are not inherent, but learned from life experiences, it follows that a moderator training course should be considered as a life experience.

Increasing Moderator Competence

The qualities of effective moderators are found in the area of self-acceptance, acceptance of others, communication, and self-awareness. All these areas are intimately linked, and to paraphrase Galileo, people cannot be taught "things"; they can only be helped to find what they know within themselves. A high level of competence in these areas reflect maturity and can occur either "naturally' (though never without conscious effort) or as the result of an educational intervention. In order to increase competence in these areas, lectures, exercises and games focusing on meditation, self-discovery and communication were designed for the training course.

Meditation

Meditation, defined as simultaneously increased levels of relaxation and concentration plays a crucial role in the development of self-awareness. Meditation reduces the anxiety which keeps people from "looking in the mirror", but at the same time sharpens the perception which is necessary in order for them to become aware of self and others through the focus of attention (see for example Bandler and Grindler 1994, Portman and Schneider 1992, Luther and Maaß 1994).

A deep insight into the conditions that shape perceptions and reactions is the basis for self-acceptance. Meditation facilitates a relaxed and understanding attitude which is necessary in order to begin or to continue the process of self-discovery. The state of consciousness achieved through meditation deepens understanding of personal behaviour patterns, which is the basis for more effective interaction. The regular practice of meditation helps people to stay focused when engaging in verbal and non-verbal communication.

Self-discovery

Communication fails whenever defence mechanisms are used. Communication can be improved through understanding the nature of defence mechanisms and their function in psychological survival. People need positive attention in order to grow physically and mentally. Self-esteem, essential for mental and even physical health, is developed by the special attention received from others; e.g., "getting strokes". To obtain or maintain the energy gained from positive attention, people develop patterns of interaction based on unique character predisposition and the specific circumstances of their lives.

> Positions are become fixed surprisingly early, from the second or even the first year to the seventh year of life ... it is not difficult to deduce from an individual's position the kind of childhood he must have had. Unless something or somebody intervenes, he spends the rest of his life stabilizing his position and dealing with situations that threaten it: by avoiding them, warding off certain elements or manipulating them provocatively so that they are transformed from threats into justifications (Berne 1964:46).

Educational intervention aims to explore and understand 1) the circumstances in each individual's life that gave rise to the development of particular defence mechanisms and 2) the current pattern of commonly used defence mechanisms. In the training course, emphasis was given to the use of gentle, appreciative and sympathetic techniques of childhood explorations. These techniques are less time-consuming, less painful, more fun and therefore more productive in this context than those used in, for example, the more clinical and often painful methods of Freudian psychoanalysis[1].

Communication

The basis of effective communication requires a satisfactory degree of self-awareness in at least one of the moderators in the focus group. For example, when group communication becomes unfocused, it is the task of the moderator to intervene. This intervention must be non-judgemental, a communication quality which can be produced only if the moderator possesses a mature level of self-awareness and self-esteem. Effective communication skills can be acquired through self-discovery and sensitivity training in the area of self-perception and perception of others. In her practical guide for effective communication, Birkenbihl (1997) designates the concept of self-esteem as a major underlying factor which strongly influences verbal expressions and reactions – and therefore, communication. Moderators-in-training need to be aware of their own "self-portrait", the threat that communication may involve, and the defence mechanisms which may result.

In the training course, students were asked to examine non-productive or dysfunctional communication patterns, beginning with themselves; e.g., how they communicate and why they communicate in the way that they do. Goals included refining their sense of perception and allowing room for the examination of relevant experiences and critical inquiries. Interactive exercises, such as those described by Luther and Maaß (1994:106-135) and Birkenbihl (1997:60-71), were used to assist students to gain competence in communication.

Linguistic style (Tannen 1989) and body language including gestures and facial expression (Fast 1971) were also discussed in the course. Both can create misunderstandings and hurt feelings. Awareness and perception are necessary to understand and successfully apply the concept of linguistic style as developed by Tannen (1989). People use their own personal style according to their momentary need for solidarity and autonomy. As these needs are contradictory though persisting to varying degrees at the same time; first, all linguistic choices for expressing the state of mind of the speaker will be incomplete, and second, they will most likely injure one of the same paradoxical needs of the listener. In spite of all best intentions, misunderstandings are an unavoidable part of verbal interaction and need to be perceived as such. Thus, it is important to learn not only what was said, but was intended to be said. In analyzing communication, it is not important what is said but what is understood.

Training for Communication with Children

Skills for communication with children were included in the training course; in particular, 1) how to establish contact, 2) how to apply various question techniques, and 3) how to give "neutral but supportive" feedback. Towards the end of the course the students conducted three focus groups with children about asthma which were videotaped in full. The videos were critically evaluated and served as the basis for further training in interactional skills.

The first contact

Moderators need to appreciate fully and accept focus groups as events which are both structured and fluid. Their goal is to provide a framework in which children perceive their creativity as essential for the successful outcome of the session.

From the first contact, it has to be clear that the moderators are open and accepting towards all the children, but are not willing to deny their own thoughts and reactions.

The way that moderators introduce themselves influences the way focus group interaction develops. In focus groups with children, the moderators have the task of projecting unconditional respect for and acceptance of the children's "word" right from the beginning. In order to convey warmth and empathy, moderators must perceive how the children feel and what they think in order to give them sympathetic verbal and, more essentially, non-verbal feedback. Children, especially, cannot and must not be fooled in this regard.

Question Techniques

Question techniques were part of the regular curriculum for moderator training, using practical guides from Birkenbihl (1997:258-270). When working with children, moderators need to have a particular appreciation of these techniques in order to avoid falling into the "teacher trap". They must avoid rehearsed questions and praising parroted answers, or overreacting to "wrong" or "right" answers.

The students developed games for the focus groups which not only provided ample intellectual satisfaction for the children but also enhanced their physical and social well-being. This success was achieved through movement and physical exercise, the exchange of mutual knowledge, and the creation of a sense of solidarity amongst the children.

Authentic feedback

Effective communication depends on positive feedback between the interacting partners. Without feedback any communication would either "run wild" or terminate. Although feedback is essential in any type of communication, it is even more crucial in focus groups, particularly those with children. Independent of the participants' ages, focus groups are an "unnatural" way of communicating and interaction requires special stimulation. Adults can understand the ultimate purpose of a focus group more easily and motivate themselves to contribute to the discussion in a constructive way. Children are in greater need of constant encouragement and motivation through feedback, as well as non-directive guidance; thus, moderators need to know how to provide different types of feedback effectively to children[2].

Authentic feedback requires recognition of what is taking place at an emotional level, and results in making the communication transparent, and therefore more objective. It is difficult to find the balance between authentic and "neutral" or "positive" feedback. Children may perceive that they are in an inferior status to the adult moderators, and "naturally" may seek affirmation about the correctness of their answers and credibility of what they say from the moderators rather than from their peers. However, the authenticity which is possible in communication between adults may need to take a different form when the communication is between adults and children. For example, when an adult says to a child, "That was a really stupid thing to say", it could result in the total withdrawal of the child from further interaction. To avoid this, it is better to use a neutral response, such as, "I'm not so sure what I think ... Let's ask the other children to talk about what you said".

Evaluation of the Training Course

Evaluating this unique experience of training undergraduate students as moderators for focus groups with children highlights the following aspects:
1) the concept of the training course;
2) the evaluation of the students;
3) the perceived success of this kind of training course.

The concept

The concept of the training course was based on a broad orientation which encompassed a variety of applications considered essential to facilitate effective communication. The content was theoretical as well as practical, drawing upon many different sources in both academic and applied sciences. While the structure of the course was well defined, there was ample space for the inclusion of the special needs, interests and talents of individuals and the specific group of student trainees.

Student reactions

The students were very motivated to improve their communication skills as so to be able to conduct focus groups with children. Initially, they hoped to acquire the required knowledge only through lectures and assigned readings. Once they realized the rationale for the more active methods of knowledge acquisition proposed in the course, they participated freely and wholeheartedly in the games and exercises. After two or three sessions, the participants were open to new experiences and towards each other. The students reported that there was a good working climate and group cohesion.

Most students found it relatively easy to understand the theory of the course. At times, however, they became frustrated with the wide range of literature they had to work through. The workload was simply too much to complete within the given period of time. Reading was relatively easy for the students; "doing" was not. While the instructor was in the lead in teaching moderation and communication competence and the students performed the more passive part, roles were reversed when it came to the actual focus groups. The students conducted the focus groups by themselves, relying on what they had learned during the course. Furthermore their knowledge in child development helped them to design games which put the children at ease and/or encouraged them to speak. When preparing the focus groups, the students asked for the instructor's help only when needed – which happened very rarely.

By the end of the course the students reported that they felt adequately trained to perform the task required of them in the focus group research project. However, they were more interested in the practical application of what they had learned from the training course in their future careers.

The results

In general, the focus groups conducted by the students with up to six children, focused on knowledge about and experiences with asthma, were successful. The children expressed their views and attitudes towards the given topic freely. They interacted with each other and the moderators in an open, spontaneous and constructive way. From the children's verbalizations and their behaviour, meaningful knowledge concerning children and asthma could be generated. The focus groups themselves helped the children to become aware of their coping strategies concerning asthma, to develop solidarity and to experience new ways of feeling and thinking about their disease.

Recommendations

Moderating focus groups with children requires a specific training which should include:

- General moderation theory and practices, improvement in communication skills and self-discovery.
- Knowledge about children's specific needs and communication potential.

From the experience of developing the moderator training course, the following suggestions are made for the planning of future courses:

- Theoretical orientation: general theory about communication and moderation, specific theory related to children's communication, techniques for moderators-in-training to improve interactive skills.
- Practical exercises aimed at the integration of theoretical knowledge through the use of games and exercises; e.g., role-playing, relaxation techniques.
- Application of theoretical knowledge and practical experience to the conduct of focus groups with children.
- Critical evaluation of the focus groups with particular emphasis on the students' interactive techniques and skills – conducted by the course organizer with the student-moderators.

Endnotes

[1]The theoretical background of this section of the training course was based on a work of Groff (1988) and Macy (1991). Excellent exercises on this material can be found in Chapter 6 of the *Experimental Guide to the Celestine Prophecy* (Redfield and Adrienne 1995). The transactional analysis developed by Berne (1964) is a brilliant tool to gain insight into personal defence mechanism patterns and those of communicational partners, complemented by the work of Harris (1970).

[2]From 1939 onwards, the psychologist Carl R. Rogers developed systematic feed-back techniques for therapeutic use (Rogers 1952). Today his approach is part of the curriculum for the training of most professionals working with people (psychologists, anthropologists, medical doctors, lawyers, social workers). Chapter 10 of *Client-Centred Therapy* (1951) provides basics about the training of counsellors and therapists which is very useful for moderators working with children.

References

Berne E 1964. *Games People Play: The basic handbook of transactional analysis.* Ballantine Books, New York.

Birkenbihl V 1997. *Kommunikationstraining.* MVG-Verlag, Landsberg am Lech.

Bandler R and Grindler J 1994. *Neue Wege der Kurzzeit-Therapie*. Junfermann, Paderborn.

Bornstein MH and Lamb ME (eds) 1992. *Developmental Psychology: An advanced textbook.* Erlbaum, Hillsdale, New York.

Debus M 1995. *Methodological Review. A handbook for excellence in focus group research.* Academy for Educational Development, Washington DC.

Doppler K and Lautenburg Ch 1995. *Den Unternehmenswandel gestalten* [trans of *Change Management*]. Campus Verlag, Frankfurt.

Fast J. 1971. *Korpersprache* [trans of *Body Language*]. Rowolt, Reinbeck.

Grof S 1988. *The Adventure of Self-Discovery.* State University of New York Press, Albany, New York.

Harris A 1970. *I´m OK-You `re OK.* Pan Books, London.

Keller H (ed) 1998. *Lehrbuch Entwicklungspsychologie.* Huber, Bern.

Luther M. and Maaß E. 1994. NLP *Spiele-Spectrum. Basisarbeit.* Junfermann Verlag, Paderborn.

Maaß E and Ritschl K 1997. *Teamgeist.* Junfermann Verlag, Paderborn.

Macy J 1991. *World as Lover, World as Self.* Parallax Press, Berkeley, California.

Maslow AH 1970. *Motivation and Personality.* Harper and Row, New York.

Portmann R and Schneider E 1992. *Spiele zur Entspannung und Konzentration.* Don Bosco, München.

Redfield J and Adrienne C 1995. *The Celestine Prophecy: An Experimental Guide.* Bantam Books, Toronto.

Rogers CR 1951. *Client-Centered Therapy.* Houghton Mifflin, Boston.

Rogers CR 1952. *Communication: Ist Blocking and Facilitation.* Northwestern University Information, USA.

Tannen D 1989. *The Argument's Cultural.* Random House, New York.

Thomann Ch, Schulz F, Thun V 1988. *Klärungshilfe.* Rowolt, Reinbeck.

Recruiting Participants and Forming Focus Groups
Ethical considerations in selecting children

Rolf Wirsing

This chapter discusses the ethical and methodological issues related to the recruitment of focus group participants and offers practical solutions for the technical challenges that need to be addressed in planning for their formation. Recruitment implies a strategy to locate individuals, as well as foresight about the intricacies involved in bringing several people together in a group discussion. The process of actually forming the groups may stimulate a reconsideration of questions about individual rights, consent, privacy, anonymity and other ethically- and methodologically-derived meanings and understandings.

Compared with preparation for other methods of data collection, such as survey questionnaires or interviews, recruitment of focus group participants is indeed a complex process and this should not be underestimated. David L Morgan, one of the forefathers of focus group methods, emphasizes that recruitment is the single most common source of failure encountered in focus group research, stating that too few people might show up and that "... all the time, money, and effort that went into recruitment may have been wasted" (Morgan 1995:517). Virtually all focus group manuals address recruitment strategies (Debus 1995, Krueger 1994, Morgan 1993, Stewart and Shamdasani 1990), but they rarely present the technicalities of recruiting children, or the particular ethical and safety considerations which must be taken into account when forming focus groups with children. Some of these issues include:

- ♦ Locating the children
- ♦ Support organizations and sponsor agencies
- ♦ Inclusion criteria and group composition
- ♦ Invitations

♦ Participant consent and ethics

Locating the Children

Most methods for locating and recruiting adults for focus groups are unsuitable for children. For example, Krueger (1994:82) suggests that the use of client rosters and employee lists is a "fast and economical" way to locate potential group participants. Marketing research organizations also have extensive resources and, for a price, provide their services by telephone contacts and door-to-door surveys to identify people who would be willing to participate in focus groups. However, children's names do not appear on such lists, nor are they usually listed in telephone directories or posted on mailboxes and doorbells. For ethical and legal reasons, children must not be approached in public places and asked to participate in research. Indeed, in contemporary societies where children are continually warned to beware of strangers, researchers approaching children on streets or playgrounds could even be suspected of attempted child molestation or drug dealing.

Public announcements

Using the mass media to advertise adult focus groups, and thereby recruit participants, is often suggested, and considered successful when incentives such as material imbursements are stated (Krueger 1994:86). In the case of locating children participants, public announcements could be posted in areas which they frequent and where they are accompanied by adults; e.g., supermarkets, youth clubs, swimming pools, schools. The announcements should list essential information about the research focus and the affiliation of the research team, and provide contact telephone numbers or addresses for parents. This method allows for the participant (in this case, the parent of the participant) to make the first contact with the research team.

It is expected that the permission of establishments and organizations to post the announcement is secured, and that adults who are involved in them are fully informed about the research. Further, the announcements should state that interested children should ask their parents to make the contact with the research team, which will not accept telephone calls from legal minors. Even if all precautions are taken, the ramifications of this seemingly non-intrusive method of locating children must be carefully considered. Aside from the fact that it may not be as successful as announcements aimed at adults, it may provoke negative reactions – particularly in an era when advertising is never what it seems to be; e.g., people selling books and periodicals use tactics which begin with a questionnaire at the front door.

Incentives

Providing material incentives for children focus group participants is not mentioned in the literature with the exception of one study with school-aged children in the United States (Menacker et al. 1999). The parents who bring the children to the group and the children themselves could easily "accept a better invitation or ... decide to relax at home rather than attend a focus group" (Morgan 1995:518). Market researchers typically solve this problem with cash payments, free products, transportation and overnight hotel accommodation (Stewart and Shamdansani 1990:56). Social scientists without such deep pockets must rely on non-monetary rewards; for example, by scheduling the focus group in conjunction with other activities which are attractive to children or by advertising the event as a chance to meet with other children.

Research budgets should include funding requests for small material rewards for focus group participants. Incentives do not need to be elaborate and overly attractive; otherwise parents might be bombarded by their children's repeated requests to participate in the project in order to get their "prizes". Posters, t-shirts and head caps are appropriate as incentives for children's focus groups. These items may be supplied by sponsors and supporters of the research; however, caution should be exercised when slogans and logos appear on the items.

Parents of children with a health problem usually respond favourably to an invitation for their children to participate in a focus group discussion where the results of the research directly involve them. Parents could also be invited to participate in a self-help group, scheduled in conjunction with the children's group, to discuss their concerns and exchange information about their child's health problem with other parents and specialists. An additional motivational factor for parents is their hope that their children might benefit from talking with the group moderators and comparing health information and illness experiences with other children.

Children are more likely to be won over if the focus group is portrayed as an exciting event that will include games and offer chances to play with other children and talk to adults interested in their opinions. Small material incentives, such as the promise of receiving snacks, toys or a t-shirt may work as additional stimuli. Children who benefit in such a way may later feel sufficiently rewarded and happy to have participated in a focus group.

Parent gatekeepers

Children's rights and child protection laws require that at least one adult gatekeeper, a parent or guardian, be consulted before children are invited to participate in research. Telephone surveys directed at children's parents preserve this ethical issue, and also appear as a recruiting technique in adult focus group manuals. In areas of the world where there is a high density of telephones, interviews-by-phone are commonplace and telephone surveys were, at one time, successfully used in marketing and social science research. However, public acceptance of telephone surveys has declined in recent years, perhaps related to tactics where seemingly innocent questions result in special sale schemes. Further, the method is labour intensive and needs a high operating budget for telephone recruiters.

The personal networks of the researchers may be utilized to avoid the intrusion of a strange voice on the telephone. Often members of the research team are either parents themselves, or have friends or relatives with young children, with whom they can easily discuss the need to find children participants. The social network of the researchers can serve as a starting point for the recruitment of children, followed by "snowball sampling"; i.e., parents who agree that their children participate in the research are asked to suggest other parents who would be willing to do the same.

Other gatekeepers

When children are selected on the basis of a particular health history, such as asthma, it is usually necessary to involve additional gatekeepers; for example, physicians and staff of therapeutic or rehabilitative institutions, along with their respective ethical committees. To maintain medical confidentiality, the parents of potential participants must be contacted first by the physicians or other health professionals. Thus, researchers must be prepared to devote time to discussing the research with a series of gatekeepers; beginning with physicians and their clinic staff, followed by parents and perhaps child advocate organizations, before finally reaching the participants -- the children.

The experience of conducting focus groups with children during the *Living with Asthma in Childhood* project (ASPRO2) provides a number of insights into the role of the "chain of gatekeepers" necessary. The following section addresses the use of sponsors, support organizations, and other intermediaries in terms of their contribution to the success of research which requires their collaboration.

Support Organizations and Sponsoring Agencies

Sponsoring agencies are defined here as those which contract the research team, fund the data collection and provide economic incentives for the participants. They often have a vested interest in the results of the research; e.g., that it will provide results which favour their educational or health care policies. Support organizations provide liaisons between the researchers and the study group. They include formal and informal groups such as parent-teacher organizations, self-help groups and health education programmes, which are favourably disposed to the research and offer services, such as providing contacts with parents and children and offering facilities for the focus group sessions. Schools play groups and weekend children's clubs (Green and Hart 1999) can also be useful as liaison groups. Collaboration with sponsors and supporters presupposes that these groups will observe all of the ethical standards of anonymity and confidentiality, and ensure that children's rights are respected and protected.

The ways in which these organizations help in locating children and interact with the research team include:

- Providing names, addresses and telephone numbers of parents and their children to the research team.

- Making initial contacts with parents and children, and if desirable and possible, scheduling focus group times and places.

- Arranging time and place for research team members to meet with children and parents in the organization (clinic, health education programme, etc.) in order to discuss the research and recruit participants.

Researcher control of focus group candidate lists

For methodological reasons, it is essential that the research team maintains control of the recruitment and selection process by setting exact specifications about the characteristics of the participants. Friends and benefactors of sponsoring agencies should be avoided in this process, particularly those who are over-enthusiastic or have conflicting interests (Krueger 1994:81). The researchers should be aware that a support organization may be unintentionally biased in suggesting candidates for focus groups. For example, health educators from an asthma summer camp may suggest only those children who exemplify the success of their programme; or health personnel from a collaborating clinic may suggest children with the best therapeutic outcome and medical compliance record. Alternatively, they may refer their more "difficult cases" in the hope that these children will benefit from additional attention. Researchers need to encourage randomization by stressing that children with a wide range of socio-economic and health care characteristics need to be included in the study.

Hypothetically, the least complicated and most methodologically sound method of locating children through support organizations is for the research team to request the names, addresses and telephone numbers of all the children and parents who use the services of the organization. This provides the research team with the greatest amount of control in selecting the participants for each focus group based on the aims of the research, and taking into account factors such as age, gender, and geographic distance from the site of the event. However, issues of confidentiality arise when the target population has a health or legal history central to the research. Physicians cannot provide lists of children who suffer from asthma; lawyers cannot disclose names of child abuse victims. In such cases, officials of the support organization must serve as the initial contact persons with the children and their parents.

Practical considerations in collaborating with clinics

The case load of clinicians competes with the time they need to locate children from their medical records, discuss the results of contacts with children and parents with the researchers, and schedule the focus groups. Even though clinical physicians may understand and endorse the aim of qualitative research about health, they may not support it wholeheartedly if they have the impression that no one in the research team understands their language or the life and death medical issues that they address every day. They want to know how the research results will improve their practice of medicine and affect the lives of their patients. While they may be pleased that articles might be published in the future, citing their name and that of their clinic, they are more interested in the immediate relevance of their participation.

These potential obstacles can be ameliorated by fairly simple but thoughtful decisions, for example:

- Including physician(s) and nurse(s) on the research team from the beginning of the study (e.g., during its methodological development) to assist in the recruitment logistics and alleviate interactional tensions which may arise between clinicians and researchers.

- Negotiating with clinic staff to allow members of the research team to be present to meet children and parents once the initial contact has been made by the physician (or other clinic personnel), and then to take over the responsibility of scheduling the groups and answering questions about the research.

- Arranging follow-up activities which include clinic staff; e.g., presentation of the study results with the staff, discussions between parents, clinicians and researchers addressing parental and children's concerns.

These suggestions have positive dimensions for both the clinic personnel and the research team. At the methodological level, the "pre-selection" of participants by the support organization is avoided and the research team has a greater degree of control over the process. At the practical level, the clinic staff is relieved of the paper work, review of files, telephoning, and other tasks which recruitment demands. Both groups can view each other "in action" and gain a clear understanding of their respective concerns and goals; e.g., the researcher learns more about the pressures of the clinic, the clinical staff learns more about the research concerns.

Focus Group Inclusion Criteria and Group Composition

The goals of a research project determine not only the type of information that is sought, but from whom it is elicited. This is a crucial element in focus groups as a method of data collection and prescribes the criteria that participants must meet in order to be selected and invited. Formulating the inclusion criteria on the basis of research goals may seem to be a fairly routine procedure; for example, if the group is expected to concentrate on experiences with asthma, it is logical that participants will be selected according to whether they have moderate to severe asthma, or are siblings of children with the condition. However, there are special considerations which must be taken into account when the members of the group are children; in particular, the size of the group, the issue of familiarity between participants, and the homogeneity of the group in terms of the age and gender of the participants.

Group size

The adult focus group literature suggests a variety of configurations for the number of participants; e.g., 4-10 (Frey and Fontana 1991), 4-12 (Wilson 1997) and 8-12 (Asbury 1995). In contrast to the upper limits of 10 to 12 adult participants, children's focus groups can and should be smaller. Experience from ASPRO2 indicates that six children in a focus group is a satisfactory target number, a figure which is supported by other focus group research with children (Frankland and Bloor 1999, Green and Hart 1999). One main consideration is that children may be hesitant to discuss sensitive topics, such as an illness, in front of a large group of other children. In practical terms, the larger the group, the more distracted, overactive or shy the children become. Further, if the group is too large, more formal rules for discussion have to be instituted such as raising a hand for permission to talk (Green and Hart 1999:30).

Small groups are suitable when participants are considered to be experts on the topic under discussion. Children are good historians and story tellers when asked to discuss their experiences with chronic illness; even if they are "novices" at the beginning of the session, by the end they can be considered as experts (Ireland and Holloway 1996:60). The children in ASPRO2, with a life-long history of asthma, emerged as experts on matters related to the management of their disease; after all, they were often involved in the intricacies of its care on a daily basis and familiar with the consequences of good and bad asthma management. Keeping children's focus groups small gives the young experts sufficient time to say what they feel is important and a chance to respond in greater depth to the comments of the others in the group (Debus 1995:13).

There are also logistic considerations in selecting a small group size; e.g., succeeding in getting more than six children in one place at one time for a focus group gathering is rarely easy. An effective way to encourage children to actually show up for a group is to schedule it to precede or follow another activity such as a party or athletic event. This method of "piggy-backing" was used by some of the local teams in ASPRO2, where focus groups were organized in conjunction with interactional asthma training courses for children and with parental asthma seminars. While piggy-backing helps to ensure participants for the focus group, the sessions are pre-programmed; thus, attention needs to be given to the possibility that piggy-backing may erode the quality of the group interaction

(Krueger 1994). In children's focus groups, this may appear in the form of "too much" familiarity between the children; e.g., friendships resulting from the adjacent activity which may develop into close-knit dyads and interfere with the interaction of the total group.

Finally, over-recruiting is the "final line of defence in recruitment strategies" (Morgan 1995:518). The rule of thumb is to invite at least two more potential participants than needed; invite a total of eight children to get possibly six. The probability that all of the invited children will come is minimal compared to the risk of having to cancel a "group" of two.

Familiarity between participants

The literature about adult focus groups usually describes them as groups which are formed to bring strangers together to discuss a particular issue (Krueger 1994:87). Specialists in child development express concern that children may have difficulties in adapting to and interacting within the context of "strangers", where all the other participants are unfamiliar to them, including the adult moderators who may be viewed as powerful figures by the children.

Green and Hart comment on the positive effects of bring peers together in group discussions, "ideally with relationships which pre-exist to the session" (Green and Hart 1999:21). However, it remains a point of contention whether children discuss and interact "better" in a group of children and moderators who they already know, or if children's focus groups should be constructed according the guidelines for adult groups. Clearly children who are not acquainted with each other before the session begins need time to "warm up" to the situation, possibly assisted by introductory games. The experience of ASPRO2 indicates that young children, and even shy ones, can be "brought into" the focus group, providing that the methods of interaction are child-centred. (See the articles of Anderson, and of Vega and Aramburuzabala, this volume).

Being acquainted with each other helps children to feel more at ease in the presence of unfamiliar moderators. However, relations of friendship and kinship may involve ingrained interactional patterns that may lead to overlooking or hiding personal information; thus, because of familiarity between the children, very little may be revealed to the moderator. Previously formed close relations between some of the children in the group may also work against the dynamics of the focus group.

The experiences of the German ASPRO2 research team may provide some insight into the question of "familiar" or "stranger". The children who participated in the focus groups had previously attended highly interactional asthma training courses. The moderators noticed that superior-subordinate relationships between group members had already been formed and may have led to the reluctance of the children from the subordinate faction to speak freely or to express negative observations in front of the more dominant children. Friendships and antagonisms developed during the training course may have prompted both supportive and negative interactions during the focus groups.

Homogeneity: Age and gender

Adult focus groups may include participants from several age cohorts because it is assumed that a range of ages will not seriously interfere with their ability and desire to engage in discussion. While forming reasonably homogeneous focus groups is usually suggested as a solid strategy, diversity can help to maximize the exploration of the focal topic from different perspectives (Kitzinger 1995). In contrast, when planning children's focus, the question of whether to aim at a high degree of homogeneity requires special consideration, particularly with respect to the age and gender composition of the group.

Children communicate best when among their peers, and in scheduling focus groups attention needs to be given to making sure that the groups do not include a wide variation in the children's ages (Green and Hart 1999). An age difference of even two years can have a significant impact on the communicative dynamics of the group. Seven year-olds often find it "awesome" to be asked to speak with 12 year-olds; older children may feel it is beneath their dignity to participate in focus groups which includes considerably younger children.

It is also important to consider gender; although this is not crucial for groups composed of seven and eight year-olds, it becomes increasingly important for older children. Eleven year-old girls may object to being assigned to a group with boys of the same age, or vice versa. There are no fast and easy rules as to where to draw the age-gender line; thus, in the planning of focus group composition it is a good idea to involve developmental psychologists, educators, and anthropologists with experience in research about children in a cross-cultural perspective. Aside from opinions of specialists concerning the homogeneity of age and gender in focus groups, the opinion of the children should also be considered. For example, they may differentiate themselves according to the school they attend, their academic grades, their preferences about leisure time activities and other variables which they use in much the way that adults define "social class" or their tennis club members.

Invitations to Focus Groups

The invitation to participate in a focus group can usually be handled by a verbal message; e.g., by telephone, after a clinic visit or school parent-teacher consultation – the standard procedure used by most ASPRO2 local research teams. If parents request a written invitation, it is important to pay attention to the details of the letterhead which symbolically attest to the seriousness, responsibility and credibility of the research team. Invitations, verbal or written, explain the purpose of the research and what takes place during a focus group with children. They point out the possible immediate benefits for each participating child but also future benefits for all children. They specify that the safety of the child and the anonymity of the family will be preserved. Invitations should emphasize that the children will not be psychologically tested or medically examined, clarify the voluntary nature of the focus groups and provide reassurance that non-attendance in no way affects the children's future medical treatment with their physician. Finally, the letter of invitation should include the name, telephone number and address of the contact research person.

Participants should receive their invitations at least two weeks in advance of the scheduled focus group date, with a follow-up telephone reminder a week later. Parents need to be asked if the chosen date and time agrees with their schedule, since they usually have to transport the child to the designated location. It is wise to telephone the parents again the day before the session, remind them about the location and time and, ask about their children's intent to attend. This extra effort reinforces the importance of their participation in the focus group. Further, if someone is unable to attend, it may still not be too late to locate and invite a substitute – a reason why keeping a list of alternates is encouraged.

Participant Consent

Focus group organizers usually approach parents before they discuss the research with the children participants. Parents, as their children's gatekeepers, must be asked for their informed consent, however this "does not negate the moral obligation of asking children for their agreement" (Ireland and Holloway 1996:157). In addition to parental consent, the children also should be asked for their agreement to participate.

Children's consent is undoubtedly influenced by how parents understand the focus group context. Parents may feel apprehensive about allowing their child to participate in a group where the moderators and other children are likely to be strangers. Some parents may have developed notions that their child is going to be tested (e.g., for learning difficulties, behavioural problems, medical conditions) during the focus group. Thus, they may expect that moderator has the proper credentials as diagnostician before granting permission, or withhold consent for fear that the evaluation will be negative. Finally, as was the case with ASPRO2, some parents may be reluctant to agree to their child's participation in a group because they view it as socially stigmatizing; they do not want their child to be "part" of a stigmatized group.

Sometimes parental consent and children's agreement to participate (or not) in a focus group are in contradiction. Parents might unintentionally coerce an unwilling child to participate because they view the focus group as an important educational activity or social event. On the other hand, a child may desperately want to be part of the activity, a member of the peer group, but the parents tenaciously withhold their consent. Fortunately these examples of conflicting "consent" are the exception rather than the rule, but when they do occur, the "rule" should give priority to the children's voice. Discretion, sensitivity and an abiding respect for the rights of children on the part of the researchers are essential in negotiating in favour of the children's wishes. These behaviours and values of the moderators are important for all the levels of working with children's focus groups.

References

Asbury JE 1995. Overview of focus group research. *Qualitative Health Research* 5(4): 414-420.

Debus M 1995. *Methodological Review: A Handbook for excellence in focus group research.* Academy for Educational Development, Washington DC.

Frankland J and Bloor M 1999. Some issues arising in the systematic analysis of focus group materials. In: *Developing Focus Group Research: Politics, theory and practice*, RS Barbour and J Kitzinger (eds). Sage Publications, London.

Frey JH and Fontana A 1991. The group interview in social research. *The Social Science Journal* 28(2): 175-187.

Green J and Hart L 1999. The impact of context on data. In: *Developing Focus Group Research: Politics, theory and practice*, RS Barbour and J Kitzinger (eds). Sage Publications, London.

Green J 1997. Children's talk about accidents. *Sociology of Health and Illness* 19(4): 457-479.

Ireland L and Holloway I 1996. Qualitative health research with children. *Children and Society* 10: 155-164.

Kitzinger J 1995. Introducing focus groups. *British Medical Journal* 311: 299-302.

Krueger RA 1994. *Focus Groups: A practical guide for applied research.* Sage Publications, Newbury Park.

Menacker F, Aramburuzabala P, Minian N, Bush PJ, Bibace R 1999. Children and medicines: What they want to know and how they want to learn. *Journal of Social and Administrative Pharmacy* 18(1): 38-52.

Morgan DL 1993. *Successful Focus Groups: Advancing the state of the art.* Sage Publications, Newbury Park.

Morgan DL 1995. Why things (sometimes) go wrong in focus groups. *Qualitative Health Research* 5(4): 516-523.

Stewart DW and Shamdasani PN 1990. *Focus Groups: Theory and practice.* Sage Publications (Applied Social Research Methods Series), London.

Wilson V 1997. Focus groups: A useful qualitative method for educational research? *British Educational Research Journal* 23(2): 209-224.

Focus Group Settings and Ambiance
Maximizing interaction, minimizing distance

Anastasia Topalidou, Aspasia Menaxiadi, DJ Trakas

The general "pleasantness" of the focus group environment influences rapport between its members (Stewart and Shamdasani 1990:34); the setting should be "relaxed and neutral" (Krueger 1993), "non-threatening" (Wilson 1997:221), and "conducive" to interaction (Albrecht et al. 1999:58). Participants are affected by the geography of the focus group – the general location, the route to the meeting room, the ambiance of the decor. Children are sensitive to places which are not child-friendly or which have negative associations for them. Unlike most adults, children do not have their own independent transportation; thus, the location must be chosen with the needs of both the children and their parents in mind. Younger children may have difficulties in sitting for any length of time in adult-sized chairs, which reduces their attention span and makes them tense or hyperactive.

As discussed elsewhere in this volume (Anderson), focus groups are contrived events. Additional artificiality in the setting can impede the attempts of the moderators to promote a facsimile of naturalness and threaten the internal validity of the group interaction. The quality of the interaction may be compromised if confidentiality is not ensured, and features such as one-way mirrors and visitors to the group can threaten the participant's trust (Krueger 1993:69). Finally, because moderators are "artificial" leaders (Stewart and Shamdasani 1990:35), their ease within the physical environment of the focus group site should be cultivated.

The physical environment of children's focus groups is central in maximizing children's interaction and minimizing the distance between moderators and children. Based the experience of the *Living with Asthma in Childhood* project

(ASPRO2), this chapter provides practical suggestions about ways to organize and help to create ambiance for children's focus group environments.

- ♦ Selecting the location
- ♦ Scheduling the sessions
- ♦ Seating arrangements and child-friendly furniture
- ♦ Settings and styles – moderator choices
- ♦ Culture and expectations for children's behaviour

Selecting the Location

Selecting child-friendly locations for focus groups revolves around three issues: 1) neutrality and familiarity, 2) space, and 3) accessibility and transportation.

Neutrality/Familiarity

The location should be "neutral", but also carry a sensation of the "familiar". Institutional settings, such as hospitals and schools, may carry negative associations for children such as disease, painful memories, strict discipline, boredom and stereotypic behaviour expectations. Neighbourhood and cultural centres are excellent places for children's focus groups for a number of reasons: They are accessible, usually convey pleasant memories and are familiar landmarks in communities.

The use of school classrooms needs to be considered carefully because the physical environment is usually loaded with images of teacher-pupil rules for communication, and children are likely to transfer these codes into moderator-participant interactions. School classrooms tend to foster inequalities between children and adults. During lessons children must raise their hand and be acknowledged by the teacher in order to speak; they are expected to remain seated during lessons and/or ask for permission to move around the classroom, and avoid aimless "chatter" with other children. These one-way rules (they do not apply to teachers) are not emphasized in children's focus groups as they tend to interfere with the ideals of the method as an egalitarian and interactive event. However, they can be difficult to shake out of the classroom setting. When school buildings are used, it is preferable to select rooms designated for activities other than "text-book learning"; for example, the multi-purpose or after-school activity room, the gymnasium.

Moderators affiliated with hospitals and clinics may suggest that the focus groups can be scheduled in a neutral area within these premises, such as the library, the children's playroom, or the hospital day care centre. Even if not all children have painful memories of hospitals, they should not have to walk through clinic corridors in order to reach the focus group room. A few of the local ASPRO2 studies did use hospitals for focus groups, but the rooms were located in wings or buildings totally separate from therapeutic and clinical areas. In preliminary comparisons between focus groups conducted in hospitals and those taking place in other locations, the moderators did not identify striking differences in the quality and dynamics of the interactions.

Space

The availability of meeting rooms with ample space is a consideration in selecting locations for focus groups. Children's focus groups need space. Unlike adults, children cannot be expected to sit in a small meeting room and, as a warm-up activity, sip coffee while informally chatting with the moderators. Instead, they might be engaged in playing a circle game or tossing a ball with each other, introducing themselves by announcing their name or other personal characteristics at designated points in the activity. They may decide they need to run off some energy in the middle of a discussion. Fantasy and projective techniques such as role-playing and using dolls or puppets also require space for movement. (See Sanz, this volume.)

Space is also required for the moderators. Standard operating procedures for focus groups designate two moderators: One in an active capacity, the other as an observer (assistant moderator), who might be seated slightly separate from the rest of the group. In small rooms, the children may feel overwhelmed by the presence of two adults with whom they are not previously acquainted.

Space is necessary for the children's parents; they cannot be expected to stand in the hallway, tempted to discover what is happening behind the closed door. Parents are usually curious about what is happening in the group and try to see inside the children's room; they may ask to observe or express ideas that their child is being tested for psychosocial skills or intelligence. Moderators need the parents to be physically distanced from the children's room, in an area where they know they can ask questions before or after the focus group session. A second room is needed to accommodate them, preferably with nearby coffee and beverage machines, chairs, reading material, or a questionnaire requesting family background information.

The availability of other facilities central to the demands of the research design also needs to be considered; for example, rooms with two-way mirrors or multimedia equipment. Children may have ideas about the identifying characteristics of two-way set-ups, perhaps from television and movie depictions, and may be immediately suspicious of the intent of the focus group or the moderators. Viewing a video (as was done in ASPRO2) may be useful in helping to set the focus and initiate the discussion. If sessions are video-taped, the children may enjoy seeing themselves on a large screen at the end of the taping, an event which might stimulate further discussion.

Accessibility/Transportation

Focus group locations need to be centrally located and/or on major public transportation lines. Safe and inexpensive transportation to the site, also an issue with adult groups, requires special consideration in organizing children's groups. Parents may allow their older children to use public transportation; parents with younger children usually prefer to bring them themselves. In places where the family car is the major source of transportation, the availability of nearby vehicle parking facilities is a plus factor for all involved in the event – parents, children and moderators.

During the planning for ASPRO2, considerable debate followed the suggestion of using a mini-van to transport the children to focus groups. This alleviates the problem of delivering the children to the same place at the same time, and thereby avoids situations that arise with early or late arrivals (e.g., insider-outsider dynamics); however, a number of complications were anticipated. The proposal was discarded, mainly due to concerns about safety, the need for additional parental permission and obtaining road liability forms such as those issued to school bus drivers.

Scheduling the Sessions

Focus group recruiters should be prepared for scheduling difficulties (and the reasons for them), without becoming overwhelmed by the potential impediments and dismiss the idea of children's focus groups as unfeasible from the beginning. Setting the time and date for focus groups is labour intensive mainly because several contacts with the participants may be needed. (See Wirsing, this volume.) In the case of children's focus groups, the participants are contacted through their parents, creating an even more intricate scheduling process. (This is certainly a challenge to the image of focus groups, often mentioned in the literature, as a fast way to accumulate large quantities of data.). Although children must be given the opportunity to voice their opinion about joining a focus group, it is usually the parents who have the final word. For example, there were a few cases of children who expressed feeling unhappy because their parents refused to allow them to participate in the ASPRO2 focus groups; the opposite was not observed.

Cautions and solutions

The preliminary focus group schedule begins by taking into account the school programme; daily hours and holiday breaks. The pros and cons of scheduling focus groups during holidays need to be considered; for example, a winter holidays or the spring school break may seem like an ideal time to schedule a series of sessions. However, these may be times when children are intensely involved in preparations for family events and religious celebrations which usually coincide with winter and spring school vacations. Focus groups scheduled at the end of the school day may interfere with homework responsibilities and extra-curricular activities. These are hours when parents are often attending to their routines of, for example, grocery shopping or transporting other children in the family to ballet classes and athletic events. Saturdays are also hectic for most families with young children, and some of the weekend days are often reserved for religious observation and visiting members of the extended family.

One way to overcome some of the scheduling difficulties is to use the "piggy-back" technique (Krueger 1994:83), wherein focus groups are scheduled to coincide with other meaningful and enjoyable events for the participants. For children, such "happenings" could include an afternoon of arts and crafts, puppet theatre, and games. These events need not be sponsored by the research team itself, but may be activities regularly scheduled on the community calendar, some of which are designed especially to give "free time" or personal time to parents in the afternoon and weekends for household errands, shopping, holiday preparations, and so forth. One ASPRO2 team piggy-backed its focus group with "asthma training" sessions for children which included a series of interactive games and physical activities especially designed to teach them about asthma care and management.

Unexpected participants

As with adult focus groups, the number of invited participants should be a few more than the projected target for each group to compensate for no-shows.

Sometimes "too many" children show up; for example, all the invited children arrive, or siblings and friends of the invited participant come along and want to be included in the event. Parents, perhaps due to lack of child care support, may give permission for their child to participate only if another sibling be included. Some children ask for the company of a brother or sister, or request to bring a friend, as part of their consent (or assent) to participate. It is difficult to exclude these extra children once they have arrived for the event and moderators need to be prepared to react in positive ways to sudden changes in the size of the group.

One way to handle the situation is to simply welcome the extra child(ren) without further explanation to avoid, for example, singling any one out as "different" from the others. Another possibility would be to specifically invite them to participate in the group, tactfully stressing the concept of "invitation". This situation tests the capabilities of the moderator's flexibility and ability to bring the outsider into the group without paving the way for the dyad (scheduled participant and unexpected child) which does not interact with the larger whole or giving others in the group that special favours are granted to selected children.

When siblings or friends of invited participants occasionally joined ASPRO2 focus groups, moderators observed that there did not seem to be any undesirable or unfortunate effects on the functioning of the group. Usually the unscheduled participants did not have asthma, providing an opportunity to observe how children with asthma explain their symptoms, feelings and life to the "other". Logically, the presence of a sibling or friend has a positive effect on the scheduled participant, although the hypothesis was not tested. From another perspective, moderators discussed their concerns about the potential for power-related situations to develop; for example, the dyad to "take over" the group or other children to feel at a disadvantage because they did not have someone who was significant to them present. This was not observed to be the case, but the dynamics of group composition according to participant categories of stranger / friend and scheduled / unscheduled deserves more systematic attention.

Seating Arrangements and Child-Friendly Furniture

Creating a child-friendly physical environment is a major factor in setting the stage for the discussion and interaction to follow. The seating arrangements should maximize the children's sense of ease and minimize their sense of distance from the moderator. Focus group rooms need to have flexible traits; for example, those with moveable furniture are preferable to those with school desks bolted to the floor – and there is no reason to assume that children will want to stay in the same place through the session.

Age and gender considerations

Decisions about the seating arrangements are based on the age and gender composition of each focus group. Young children need furniture to suit their size, and it is important that the moderators also use the same seats and tables as the children so that they are not hovering over the children's heads. In the absence of children-sized seats, pillows or small rugs can be placed on the floor. Older children may be insulted or embarrassed by being asked to sit on pillows, particularly if the group includes 11 year-old girls and boys who are meeting for the first time. Forming a circle of chairs may also have gender-related difficulties. Ten year-old girls may feel exposed in a circle of chairs, tend to hold their arms over their chests throughout the discussion and prefer to sit around a table. In groups consisting of all boys, the pillows may be an invitation for a wide variety of activities related to using the pillows to punch and throw at each other.

Some of the ASPRO2 local teams seated the children at desks, and reported that this did not seem to impede discussion between the children and moderator. Other teams used pillows on the floor and permitted the children to circulate around the room. Moderators of these groups observed a high level of creative interaction between the children. They were pleased that this type of environment allowed them to move away from an autocratic or didactic role, and to relate to the children in an egalitarian manner; to become peripheral to the discussion rather than its pivotal point. These types of differences in interaction were clearly visible when video tapes of selected sessions were viewed by the entire ASPRO2 research group, leading to the consensus that offering relaxed seating possibilities is the more child-friendly approach. However, this is contingent on many other factors such as the ages of the children, gender distribution of the group, format of the focus group protocol, and goals of the research design.

Arranging the room and seating charts

The children, especially the early arrivals, can help in setting up the room by placing chairs, desks, tables, pillows and small rugs; thus, arranging the room forms part of the warm-up activities. Once all the children are assembled, the moderator(s) can ask them if they feel comfortable with the arrangement or would like to change anything about it. Some may decide that they want to sit in a different place -- either at the beginning or during the course of the session. Changing seats (chairs, pillows or small floor rugs) or even getting up and walking around can happen frequently in children's focus groups (and if not, children may be hoping for the possibility).

Focus group manuals usually suggest the use of a seating chart to facilitate the identification of the participants by the moderators. Notations using the seating chart can help to identify which participant is speaking on the audio-tape of the session. This system for facilitating voice recognition assumes that the participants, after selecting their seat at the beginning of the session, will stay in the same place throughout. Adults usually do not find any difficulties with this; children may feel constrained and ask to change places, thus other means of identification need to be used. Self-stick labels can be distributed and, for an introductory activity, the children can write their names on them, adding colours and designs. Warm-up activities should include "naming games"; e.g., the moderator tosses a ball and asks "What's your name?", the child who catches the ball responds by shouting out her/his name, and tosses the ball to another child asking the same question. This promotes the children's communication with each other and also helps the moderator to memorize their names.

Settings and Styles – Moderator Choices

The idea, mentioned earlier, that moderators are "artificial" leaders, needs some clarification according to different types of focus group contexts and settings. The artificial role of moderators can be balanced by a good sense of familiarity with the focus groups room, which in turn, helps the children to perceive the entire situation as natural. Moderators need to rehearse and to anticipate when and how they will move around the room; e.g., seating the participants, serving refreshments, using focus group stimulus materials such as pictures, toys, VCRs, and audio- or video-tapes. Previewing the composition of each focus group and arriving at the site early enables them to adjust the setting to suit the characteristics of the particular group.

The arrangement of the room often depends on the focus group "style" developed by the moderators. In some of the ASPRO2 local studies, the style was "formal", adhering to the format protocol by using essentially the same series of questions posed by the moderator (described by Hallia and Vaskilampi, this volume). The children usually remained in their seats throughout the session, answering most of the questions, which was the original goal of setting up the format. In other sites, a less formal approach was used; for example, role-playing activities were made central to the focus group format, sometimes assisted by toys and other props. Children's movement around the room was essential during the play segments of the session. One local team experimented with forming the entire focus group around a game-playing approach (Sanz, this volume). The implications for different room characteristics in terms of the type of seating arrangements and the use of space in the implementation of these various approaches are obvious.

The ambiance of the room and the moderators' choices about their focus group style (question-answer, role-playing, game-centred) are interrelated. In ASPRO2, moderators also made decisions about their style based on their scientific background and training, which also set the criteria for evaluating the quality of their groups. Some evaluated question-answer and essentially moderator-centred focus groups as "successful", based on the criteria that all the topics in the format were covered. Others were concerned that the groups in this category lacked interaction between the children and projected what "might" have happened if the format had been less formal; e.g., if role-playing or fantasy techniques would have been introduced, if the children had been encouraged to move around the room. In a spirit of methodological loyalty, some moderators held tenaciously to a protocol of what a focus group "must" include and how it should "work". Others were more interested in exploring what a focus group "might" include and discovering where it is possible to "go". These evaluations may also be related to cultural factors particularly with respect to expectations for children's behaviour in different settings.

Cultural and Expectations for Children's Behaviour

Decisions about location, transportation, scheduling and particularly the ambiance of the room, are functions of practical considerations. They are also related to cultural differences in expectations for children's behaviour. The issues that need to be addressed in the selection of focus group settings and ambiance require reflective thought about the local research goals and structure in order to avoid misunderstandings about focus group geography. Questions which moderators might ask in this effort include:

- Will children try to behave as ideal pupils if the focus group is conducted in a school classroom?

- Will children be frightened or feel that they should talk about illness if they participate in a focus group held in hospital premises?

- ♦ If children are allowed to sit on pillows on the floor, along with the moderators, will it promote a more egalitarian atmosphere -- or will it compromise the "role" of the moderator in the eyes of the children?

- ♦ Can it be suggested that children use public transportation to travel to the location of the session or will this come into conflict with parents' ideas about safety, independence, or risk?

- ♦ Will the session intrude on "family time" or push parents to release their children from ethnic observances or religious commitments?

- ♦ Will the attempt to create an egalitarian ambiance in the focus group setting come into conflict with cultural norms regarding the submissive (or not) behaviour of children?

In some research locations, children perceived the school (or even the hospital) as a friendly, familiar place, integrated into their neighbourhood and close to other landmarks in their life. The school was both neutral and familiar, particularly when the building was open "after hours" for use as an activity centre. In other communities, the school was geographically distant and required school bus or public transportation for children to reach; other schools were off-limits after the daily programme of instruction ended. Interactions between children and teachers may be generally democratic in some societies and repressive in others; i.e., the classroom environment itself is not the decisive factor. Consequently, there does not seem to be any reason to rule out using classrooms for focus groups.

There were striking differences between the local ASPRO2 studies related to the use of community centres and athletic facilities. Some required rental fees and bureaucratic negotiations to gain permission and/or there were restrictions on the use of the premises which interfered with experimentation with ambiance and other plans for the use of space; e.g., furniture could not be moved around, food and beverages were not allowed, equipment needed to be formally inventoried at the end of the session. However, requirements for the removal of shoes when entering a room used for dance and exercise, for example, are minor when compared to the possibilities to organize the space to meet the needs of a "spacious" focus group style. .

In study sites where older children were allowed to use public transportation on their own, the "problem" of parents waiting outside the meeting room was elimi-

eliminated. When the parents needed to be involved in the transportation, they sometimes wanted to wait right outside the meeting room to wait for the "results". However, other parents who did accompany their child to the focus group location were perfectly willing to go shopping or do errands while the group was in progress. These differences seemed to be related to cultural factors which, in turn, influence the performance of the parental role; for example, the degree to which parents are actively involved in their children's study habits and school examination results. In some societies, the cultural ideal is to allow children to organize their own study time and parents rarely accompany their children when examination results are announced. In others, the performance of the parental role includes interacting with children as they study and investing in private, after-school tutorials. As a result of this significant emotional and financial investment, parents have full rights to being present when results are posted (as well as to become involved in challenges to rankings and numerical scores).

In some ASPRO2 study sites, children were expected to spend the majority of their time during weekends and holidays with the family, and it was inappropriate to schedule focus groups in conflict with this custom. The opposite tendency was apparent in other locations; it was automatically accepted that during holidays children would be involved in many of their own activities such as camping, athletics and parties with friends.

Children, particularly when the setting is unfamiliar to them, expect adults to set and maintain the rules. Depending on their family and cultural or ethnic background, children may respond differently to rules about their behaviour in the unfamiliar situation of a focus group. In some cultures, children have strict restrictions placed upon them; for example, in their home environment they are expected to be "seen but not heard", in their schools the rules are rigid, in society their future potentials are continually weighed; autonomy is not particularly encouraged. In other cultures, children's rights reign supreme and the children themselves are very aware of them; independence is a social value. These types of culturally influenced factors need to be considered when selecting focus group locations and when developing socially harmonious settings with child-friendly ambiance. To take this one step further, it is important for moderators to cultivate a deliberate consciousness about the way in which material and cultural factors contribute to their focus group style.

References

Albrecht TL, Johnson M, Walther JB 1993. Understanding communication processes in focus groups. In: *Successful Focus Groups: Advancing the state of the art.* (A Sage Focus Edition), DL Morgan (ed). Sage, London.

Krueger RA 1993. Quality control in focus group research. In: *Successful Focus Groups: Advancing the state of the art.* Sage (A Sage Focus Edition), DL Morgan (ed). Sage, London.

Krueger RA 1994. *Focus Groups: A practical guide for applied research.* Sage, Thousand Oaks.

Stewart DW and Shamdasani PN 1990. *Focus Groups: Theory and practice.* (Applied Social Research Methods Series) Sage, London.

Wilson V 1997. Focus groups: A useful method for educational research. *British Educational Research Journal* 23(2):209-244.

Developing Focus Group Formats and Themes
An example from cross-cultural research with children

Outi Hallia and Tuula Vaskilampi

Every so often, focus group handbooks mention the possibility that children might be participants; in which case, "modifications" of adult focus group formats might be necessary. Although some point out that children have a short attention span, or have different cognitive and verbal abilities than adults (e.g., Stewart and Shamdasani 1990), there have been delays in definitive suggestions for age-appropriate focus group formats, moderator guides and discussion techniques. Specific proposals based on our participation in the early planning and piloting of the preliminary focus group format for the *Living with Asthma in Childhood* project (ASPRO2) and the pursuant collective experience of the research teams are presented in three sections:

- ♦ Planning formats for children's focus groups
- ♦ Focus themes and questions
- ♦ Focus group formats in different cultural settings

Planning Formats for Children's Focus Groups

The core of a focus group format consists of themes, lines of questioning and notations about techniques which promote interaction between the participants. These guidelines provide direction for the focus group, but before their details are drawn up, certain general operating procedures must be agreed upon between the moderators. These decisions include the format or protocol to be used for greeting the children and the creation of a child-friendly atmosphere in which young people feel free to speak up and answer questions posed by an adult and to interact with each other. Aside from communication skills and sensitivity, moderators should have considerable experience in speaking with and listening to children, a tolerance for children's activity levels, and an appreciation of the communicative talents of children.

General considerations which can help children's focus groups be productive include:

- ♦ Moderator agreements and division of labour
- ♦ Children's arrival at the session
- ♦ Introductory phase and agreement on rules
- ♦ Warm-up activities and taking breaks
- ♦ Audio-visual materials and multimedia activities
- ♦ Length of sessions
- ♦ Use of moderator worksheets

Moderator agreements and division of labour

Virtually all focus group handbooks suggest that two researchers be actively involved in the sessions. One person, the moderator, is assigned to pose questions, stimulate discussion, and keep the session focused. The other, the assistant moderator, attends to technical tasks such as operating the audiotape recorder and drawing the seating chart, makes notations about who is speaking and at which point, and takes notes on the interactions, including body language. The first is the actor and reactor; the other is the low-profile observer.

Experience with children's focus groups shows that in practice both researchers alternate responsibilities, thus, it is more exact to speak of two moderators. In reality the assistant moderator is much more than an assistant, and the active moderator tries to move to a peripheral "place" in the group. Since children's focus groups, for logistic and methodological reasons, tend to be smaller than adult groups, a natural question to ask is, maybe two moderators are too many? Children may be overwhelmed when they are asked to talk to one adult stranger; a second adult in the setting may be even more threatening. It is beneficial to have a second moderator for noting changes in the seating chart, untangling a child from a chair, taking a child to the washroom, and it is crucial that the two moderators do not present competing behaviours to the children.

Moderators may be very clear with each other about their roles before the session begins, but once the group becomes active, other scenarios may emerge to challenge the harmonious division of labour. It is important for the children to know "who is in charge"; for example, which moderator will ask the questions, which one can be asked for assistance in finding the washroom or facilities, which one will handle rambunctious or rowdy behaviour. Sometimes children might seek feedback from both adults, and moderators need to be clear with each other what happens under these circumstances. The children may be puzzled by the seemingly passive part played by the assistant moderator; for example, the children in one local ASPRO2 study where role-playing was used often, expressed concern when assistant moderators were not included in the story and initiated their own tactics to bring them into the scene.

Children's arrival at the session

Most of the literature suggests that adult focus groups should include 6 to 12 participants (Asbury 1995). The experience of ASPRO2 shows that children's groups can and should be smaller. Even so, it is unlikely that five or six children will all arrive at the same place at the same time. Moderators will want to wait until they are sure that all the invited children are present – or at least long enough to confirm that some will not attend. In the meantime, they are occupied with greeting the children who have already arrived and helping them adjust to the new situation.

Parents or older siblings may also appear on the scene and require some form of hospitable attention. To avoid complications, the children need to be invited into the meeting room immediately upon their arrival and the non-participating parents or older siblings directed to stay outside – separation tensions do not usually accompany the formation of adult focus groups. During the arrival of the children and parents at the focus group location the communication might begin to break down even before it has formally begun, particularly when the children have not previously met each other. Shy children may become even more silent and distance themselves from the group, clinging to a parent or sibling. Children who tend to bully or be strong figures in any group may be tempted to use their "talents". The moderators need to agree on gentle ways to separate the children from their parents and to anticipate possible antagonisms between the children.

Parents may want to see the focus group area, talk with the moderators, and even ask to sit in for the warm-up activities. To help parents feel that they are part of the event, and meanwhile keep them away from the meeting room, they can be asked to provide information which is useful for the research. For example, parents of the children in the ASPRO2 focus groups completed a family background questionnaire while the children were involved in the sessions. They appreciated being provided with coffee, tea and soft drinks in the "waiting room" or even the corridor. In fact, the possibility of conducting separate parallel focus groups with parents (while children were involved in their own session) was considered in the early planning of ASPRO2. From the methodological perspective, there were suggestions that this is solid reasoning (see Vega and Aramburuzabala, this volume), further it involves parents with the process and, in a sense, uses to a full extent the time and effort devoted to the intricate steps in organizing the children's groups. While some local teams held focus groups with parent, this was not included in the project-level protocol for several reasons; mainly it required additional moderators and new directions in their training, and in addition managing the children's groups was a full-time challenge.

Once they have been gathered together in the meeting room, young children usually do not spontaneously strike up conversations with other early arrivals or chat with the moderators – as might adults in a similar situation. Activities used in ASPRO2 to help the children feel that they were part of the group included:

- Writing their names on large self-adhesive labels which they can embellish with designs.
- Helping arrange the chairs or cushions for the floor; the meeting room does not have to be in perfect order when the children arrive.
- Helping set up a snack and beverage table.
- Playing a table game with the other early arrivals.
- Welcoming other children as they arrive.

Introductory phase and agreement on rules

At some point after the arrivals and the separations, the session formally begins. In the case of a late-comer, special care must be taken to welcome the child to the group (without disrupting the flow of the interaction which is being formed) and the assistant moderator will need to greet the parent in the waiting area.

As with adult focus groups, both of the moderators introduce themselves to the participants and explain the focal topic and the reason for the meeting. In children's groups, the introduction needs to be presented in age-appropriate language, but without talking down to the children. Thus, it is essential that moderators have experience in working with children in groups. The introductory statements used by the ASPRO2 moderators are quite similar to those used by Menacker and her colleagues (1999) for children's focus groups in the United States. They also echo the introductory words to the drawing-interviews with children used by researchers in the two European concerted actions which preceded ASPRO2 – suggesting the similarity in egalitarian perspectives among researchers implementing qualitative methods with children. Also significant was the collaboration of Patricia J Bush in all of the projects, the three in Europe and the one in the US (Bush et al. 1996; See the Foreword, this volume.)

- I want to learn from you.
- I hope to hear about your opinions.
- I am not your teacher -- and I am not testing you.
- You don't need to worry about right or wrong answers.

Following these introductory words, the moderators set out the general rules for the focus group interaction:

- The functioning of the group: "Everyone has a chance to talk. It's all right to interrupt me [the moderator] -- but try not to interrupt when other children are speaking. You don't have to raise your hand to talk."

- Children's desire for free movement during the session: "It's o.k. if you want to stand up and stretch, or change the place where you're sitting."

- Safety considerations: "You can leave the room if you need to use the washroom but tell me so I can help you / make sure that someone can help you."

- Ethical considerations: "You can also decide to leave the room if you don't want to participate any more, but tell me so that I can make sure someone is waiting for you and you won't be alone."

Children should be invited to express any other ideas that they might have about the codes of conduct for participation; however, since they are accustomed to seeing adults as authority figures, they may be reluctant to make suggestions. New rules may need to be introduced as the focus group unfolds; for example, when children's behaviour begins to negatively interfere with the dynamics of group interaction. Moderators need to be ready to address "small distractions" which arise in the course of the focus group; for example, when certain children continually pinch and bump each other, or make faces, grimaces, and hand gestures while others are talking. In the interest of continuity it is recommended that one of the two moderators be designated for managing these types of distractions and nuisances.

Warm-up activities and taking breaks

In adult focus groups, the introductory stage is often accompanied by serving coffee or tea, a social activity associated with extending hospitality and an occasion for small talk and chatting (even among strangers), and serves as a sufficient "warm up" for adults. Children can also be served orange juice or milk during the introductory phase, but this may not help them to "warm up" to the other participants or to the moderators. They are not used to striking up a conversation with other children over a class of lemonade.

The ASPRO2 moderators began by asking the children to introduce themselves by stating their name and age, and saying something about their family, usually about their brothers and sisters. In some local studies the introductions were incorporated into a warm-up game which usually consisted of tossing a ball between the children and moderators. Catching the ball required the statement of identifying information by the receiver – name, school, number of siblings, favourite school subjects, best friend's name, and so on. The categories for each specific type of information were decided by various democratic procedures and the game could be expanded to include other variations (see Sanz, this volume).

Taking a break from the formal activities of the session is essential with children's focus groups. When the attention of the children seems to be reaching its limit (or the patience of the moderators) it may indicate that whatever is being discussed has also reached its limit. A intermission can help children continue with the second half in a more relaxed way and moderators can "re-group" their energies. Even if the interest level of the children seems to be interactive and high, it is probably a good idea to take a "half-time" break, particularly with groups of 7 and 8 year-olds. Of course, without being able to predict how long the entire session will be, it is difficult to gauge when it has reached the middle. Generalizations about the relationship between time variables, attention span and expected length of a session according to age can be helpful. However, other factors may be equally or even more important; e.g., previously existing friendships among the participants, the intensity of a game-oriented approach, the enhancement provided by multimedia techniques.

Simple activities such as stretching, running in place or skipping around the room can constitute a break. Serving extra water or orange juice may be necessary at the end of a vigorous break. Some ASPRO2 moderators served cookies, biscuits, or chips – but found that these treats sometimes ended up being tossed around by the children. With children's focus groups, it is often during the break that important information about the children and the dynamics of the group emerge. Consequently, moderators should continue to note their observations during breaks.

Audio-visual aids and multimedia activities

Most children like to have the chance to meet with other children, but when an event is organized by adults, they may have reservations, especially if they are expected to "discuss" in front of an older person. Moderators might present a short multimedia event as an "opening attraction" before the discussion begins; for example, listening to an audiotape or CD, viewing a cartoon video, watching a puppet show. Or children could be invited to participate in drawing pictures or making clay figures. In planning these activities it is important that the activity 1) is age-appropriate, 2) helps the children feel pleasant in the meeting room, and 3) is related to the focal topic to be explored in the discussion.

In the ASPRO2 focus groups, a 15-minute cartoon video intended to educate young children about asthma and its pharmacological treatment was shown at the beginning of the session. "Oscar", as the video came to be referred to by the members of the project, was produced by a major transnational pharmaceutical company and available in several languages, conveniently including those of all the countries in the project. Discovering the video was initially considered to be a stroke of good luck, followed by reservations about ethical compromises. There was some concern as to whether using the video which could potentially be considered as an instrument to entice young focus group participants to become advertising intermediaries by telling their parents about the company's products or asking their physicians to prescribe them. It was concluded that its actual advertising content was minimal and not directed towards young viewers (e.g., the name of the company in small print under the title, at the end with the credits and acknowledgments) and the video was incorporated into the protocol.

In some local studies, the invitations to the focus groups explained to children and their parents that a cartoon video would be part of the big event. Perhaps this tactic serves as an incentive for children to participate, but it by no means secures that they will feel overjoyed when they view it or want to talk about it. Moderator evaluations about the role of the video in the session conclude that it was not particularly effective in providing a focus for the group and stimulating discussion. It did not seem to generate any strong reaction which provoked children to engage each other in a debate about its "plot", message or "action scenes". In fact, they sometimes seemed hesitant to reveal their negative – or actually neutral – reactions about the video to the moderator. The younger children seemed to be momentarily amused by the caricatures, but little else.

Part of their (lack of) reaction to the video could be related to its somewhat dated appearance; for example, the cartoon figures were conservatively depicted and somewhat "flat" – particularly compared to what is available for most young television viewers. Children in European countries usually have access to a wide variety of audio-visual adventures (ninja turtles, power rangers, pre-teen fashion icons) and multimedia events (metamorphosed creatures, lightening fast action, billowy fairyland fantasies) with much more sophisticated and exciting content than would be selected for focus group research where a "family viewing" approval is necessary. Thus, using these types of materials as a "stimulus" is probably not an option for children's groups.

Length of sessions

Focus group sessions with children run as long as the children are still willing to talk and interact; there is no rule on length. Some ASPRO2 moderators felt satisfied when the session lasted for 45 minutes, particularly with groups of 7 and 8 year-olds, and when the major topics in the thematic format had been covered. Others were disappointed with the shortness of a 45-minute session and wondered what "else" could have been done to "produce" more interaction or gain more information. The fact that the literature about adult focus groups describes them as two-hour sessions increased the anxieties of moderators that "something more" should be added to the agenda to extend the length of children's groups; however, this unease should not be over-exaggerated.

It would be counterproductive to arbitrarily add more themes to the format in the moderator guide – simply to "make" longer sessions. The length of sessions with children depends on factors related to the nature of <u>their</u> focus groups; for example, hierarchical positions between children and adults may work against children's spontaneity, children meeting each other for the first time may produce tenuous interactions, and the oft-cited short attention span of children may result in truncated discussions. Simple logistic factors can also be responsible for relatively brief sessions; children's focus groups need to be smaller than adult ones, hence there are fewer speakers, and a "round" of discussion about a given topic takes less time.

The manner in which the thematic format is implemented also relates to the session length. Even though the ASPRO2 moderator guide was identical for all local research teams, in practice, the moderators conducted their groups using different "styles". Some closely followed the format to the letter in what might be called a "conventional" style; others introduced role-playing; and still others based the entire session on games and play. The game-playing focus groups tended to be longer than the conventional ones for two reasons – the time necessary to organize the plan for the game activity and the level of the children's engagement in play. On the other hand, the goal-oriented approach of the conventional focus group allows less time for the exploration of peripheral topics, which may, in practice become central as the research unfolds. This issue is discussed in greater detail by Emilio Sanz in the next chapter.

Use of moderator worksheets

After each focus group session the moderators need to debrief each other by discussing the events which took place. The post-session evaluation can be used as a guide for the initial analysis of the focus group. The protocol for the format and the list of themes form the core of a "worksheet" which is an important part of the data management and analysis (see Trakas, this volume). Topics in the ASPRO2 worksheet included:

- Research group list: names of children and their code numbers
- Date and length of the discussion
- Audiotape number
- Description of the formation of the group: e.g., by telephone or personal contact in a clinic
- Completing planned group size: e.g., arrival order, no-shows, extra participants (friends, siblings of scheduled children)
- Synthesis of the group; age and gender of children, relationship to each other
- Family profile of each child (parent's education, occupation, size of family, etc. from a parental questionnaire)
- Sociodiagram of interactions: e.g., leaders, frequent speakers, silent participants, clusters of interaction
- Main issues discussed
- Reaction to and discussion of the video
- Positive points about the group and possible reasons for its success
- Difficulties and possible explanations

Keeping notes on each and every point is a challenge not always met; however, it is important to designate a space in all the worksheets for each topic. Simply noticing the topic or issue as the worksheet is being completed helps moderators recall more details about a focus group than they might have thought initially. For this dimension of the worksheet to function, moderators should begin organizing and creating each dossier immediately after the completion of the session.

Focus Themes and Questions

The formulation of themes and questions to be explored in focus groups is a factor which shapes the quality of the group interactions. Some of the threats to quality (Krueger 1993) are listed below, with particular attention to how these might manifest themselves in children's groups:

- ♦ Too many topics: Five to eight basic themes are more than sufficient for children's focus groups.

- ♦ Over-reliance on formal expert knowledge: When the participants have personal experience with the focal topic, such as a history of asthma, they should be listened to as "experts" (even if they are children, even in preference to medical experts).

- ♦ Questions are too abstract or so concrete that only yes/no answers result: When children are asked to talk with adults, they tend to answer in monosyllables; thus, moderators need to give special attention to the way they form questions.

Thematic format

This section presents the thematic format used in ASPRO2 as a specific example of how focus themes and questions to be asked are developed. The goals of the focus group centred on two issues:

1) How children react to and talk about the "Oscar video" which they view (together) before the main discussion.
2) How they relate the messages of the video to their own asthma experiences.

The thematic format was composed of eight topics divided into two groups:

<u>Group 1: Recall from the video</u>
1) The mechanics of asthma; e.g., lung function, physical causes
2) Asthma "triggers"
3) Asthma medicines

4) Social and physical activity

Group 2: Experiences with asthma
5) Reactions to asthma episodes; e.g., fear, discomfort
6) Recognition of "personal" asthma triggers
7) Use of asthma medicines
8) Concerns about social relationships and physical activities

Types of questions

Four types of questions were developed, beginning with those asking for children's reactions to and evaluation of the video, and followed by those about how the video relates to their experience of asthma:

- ♦ Starters
- ♦ Recall (of the video messages)
- ♦ Expansion techniques
- ♦ Interaction facilitators

Starter questions

It is a good policy to begin the discussion with loosely structured questions and proceed to more specific ones as the group interaction unfolds (Stewart and Shamdasani 1990). The starter questions in ASPRO2 inquired about the children's responses to the video:

- ♦ What did you think about the video?
- ♦ Was it interesting? Why (or why not)?
- ♦ Was there anything unusual that happened? (What was it?)

Children often said, "Eh - so it was just a video. So what? It's not as much fun as the other things we see on TV." They were mildly entertained by a walking, talking and wheezing "lung" caricature with a head on it explaining to them about "their" asthma. Nevertheless, they were waiting for the chance to talk about their own experiences, if not stimulated by the images of the video, at least related to its messages. Some of their concerns were about dust and pollen in their environment, adults smoking around them, use of inhalers, names of medicines, comparisons to children without asthma, and the desire to participate in athletics and to "be normal". These issues are consistent with those noted in focus groups conducted with children about illness (Ireland and Holloway 1996:161).

Recall questions

It was important to try to listen to how children heard and evaluated the messages of the video, in spite of its general unattractiveness to them. What did the children have to say about what they saw and heard? What did they think they learned? Questions such as the following were asked:

- ♦ What happened in the video?
- ♦ What new things did the video tell you about?
- ♦ What were the most important things you learned from the video?
- ♦ Did any of those things in the video have anything to do with you?

At this point the children begin to recall how the video messages related to what they had (or had not) already learned about their asthma episodes, care, and medication. The moderators proceeded to explore children's lived and embodied experience of asthma and used the opportunity to expanding the focus of the session.

Expansion techniques

Sources of information before the video needed to be explored; that is, the messages about asthma that children had heard from parents, doctors and other health educators. Extend the focus beyond the children's evaluation of the video messages led to asking about how messages in the video related to the children's everyday life:

- ♦ Asthma medicine use; how, when, where children use them
- ♦ Social life; sports, play during school breaks
- ♦ Perceptions about lung function and its relation to using peak flow metre (or not)
- ♦ Prevention strategies from the video; avoiding asthma "triggers", daily diaries, charting daily peak-flow meter readings
- ♦ Children's knowledge about asthma before viewing the video; sources of their information

Facilitating interaction

Children are usually willing to try to respond to the direct questions of the moderator; however, the goal of focus groups is to develop discussion between the participants rather than evaluate individual knowledge. In adult group discussions, opinions are expressed not only for the moderator to hear, but also to be "bounced off" between participants. Two or three different opinions may be expressed and "thrashed out" between the participants, often without the intervention of the moderator.

With groups of children, creating this particular type of "give and take" is difficult (see Anderson, and Vega and Arambubuzabala, this volume). Moderators can try to create the interaction by introducing questions such as:

- Does anyone else have something to say about what Jimmy just said?
- Do you agree with what Mary said?
- Is John's description (answer, idea, experience) similar to yours?
- Why do you think Anna said what she said?

Children who remain totally silent are a challenge for moderators, who tend to blame themselves for the lack of discussion. Indeed, most children seem to be motivated by the desire to say something that will please the moderator or the other children in the group. There is no way to force the non-verbal child to speak (any more than there is a way to force the very verbal child to stop speaking). The interaction in a focus group is not always verbal and here the observational skills of the moderators, particularly those of the assistant moderator, are essential. Some children are not sure about what is expected of them in a focus group – others may be puzzled about why they are in the group in the first place, having joined because a friend did, or their parents wanted them to participate based on the suggestion of their family doctor.

Focus Group Formats in Different Cultural Contexts

ASPRO2 was a cross-cultural, multidisciplinary project and the thematic format was initially outlined for use in this context. It was adjusted following the evaluation of pilot focus groups in two research locations; i.e., the piloting could neither foresee all of the possible cultural parameters which would come into play in the other study sites nor anticipate the perspectives from scientific disciplines not involved in the piloting. Some project members had reservations about the implementation of the format in a conventional manner, projecting that this would be a replication of the guidelines for adult focus groups. Others conceded that the thematic format was central for a level of standardization, but without supplementary techniques such as role-playing, the focus groups would become simply question-and-answer sessions.

In some research sites implementing the conventional-style moderator's guide was evaluated as very successful. The information generated by the focus groups fulfilled the goals of the guide and additional techniques were seen as unnecessary. However, the focus groups in these research sites included other characteristics which may have contributed to the favourable evaluation:

- Several of the children knew each other prior to the focus group.
- The children had met the moderators before the session.
- The groups consisted of "homogenous" age groups; e.g., 7 to 8.5 year-olds, or 9 to 11 year-olds.
- Children is some locations seemed more accustomed to structured, task-oriented group activities.

The scientific background of the ASPRO2 moderators may have influenced their evaluation of how well the thematic format or the style in which it was implemented "worked". Moderators accustomed to questionnaire-based research were usually pleased when the topics in the moderator's guide were covered in essentially a structured group-interview approach; i.e., children answering the moderator's questions rather than discussion between the children. Others felt that the focus groups conducted with the use of games were more productive, particularly in terms of promoting interaction between the children. Consensus was clear about one point: There is no "one" focus group style which "works best". Moderators need to prepare for each focus group based on the profile of its participants (as a unit) and be in tune with each group of children in order to implement the style which best suits them – conservative, innovative, game-playing, conversational.

Finally, cultural differences play an important role in shaping adult expectations of children's behaviour. It is assumed that children should be raised to be obedient and polite with adults; however, exactly what behaviours constitute an obedient child differs between cultures. Focus group moderators, as products of their own culture, have differing expectations as to how "their" children should behave in "their" focus groups. For example, in the Nordic countries, children should be safely asleep by early evening. In group activities, they are expected to wait quietly for their turn, and are encouraged not to interrupt a conversation.

In contrast, children in the Mediterranean countries may still be running around in the garden at eleven o'clock at night; in group activities they are inclined to avoid notions of taking turns. A "normal" discussion in Spain or Greece, when transported to Finland or Norway, may sound like one long interrupted conversation or even argument.

The cross-cultural experience of ASPRO2 reinforces the principle that formats for focus groups with children can (and should) access a number of styles. Perhaps the most important guideline to offer to planners and moderators of children's focus groups is suggest that they refer to the positive experiences of their own childhood – so as to develop focus group themes and styles of implementation which are relevant to children.

References

Asbury JE 1995. Overview of focus group research. *Qualitative Health Research* 5(4):414-42O.

Bush PJ, Trakas DJ, Sanz EJ, Wirsing RL, Vaskilampi T, Prout A (eds) 1996. *Children, Medicines, and Culture.* Pharmaceutical Products Press, Binghamton, NY.

Ireland L and Holloway I 1996. Qualitative health research with children. *Children and Society* 10:155-164.

Krueger RA 1993. Quality control in focus group research. In: *Successful Focus Groups: Advancing the state of the art*, DL Morgan (ed). Sage (A Sage Focus Edition), London.

Menacker F, Aramburuzabala P, Minian N, Bush PJ, Bibace R 1999. Children and medicines: What they want to know and how they want to learn. *Journal of Social and Administrative Pharmacy* 18(1): 38-52.

Stewart DW and Shamdasani PN 1991. *Focus Groups: Theory and practice.* Sage, London.

Creating Opportunities for Expression
Interactive games in children's focus groups

Emilio J Sanz

Most formats for conducting focus groups, independent of how sensitively or liberally they are applied by the moderator, carry implicit messages for children about adult authority and expectations about behaviour. Children are accustomed to interacting with other children within the parameters set by adults (sharing, politeness, taking turns, being fair), a model which is replicated when developing formats for children's focus groups. The moderator guide (thematic list, suggestions for implementation) developed for the *Living with Asthma in Childhood* project (ASPRO2) was successful in eliciting children's responses to specific questions and themes, but it did not insure that children would engage with each other interactively.

Children develop their own operating rules, tactics and strategies which they apply to their own agendas, preferences and standards for social behaviour (Christensen and James 2000, James 1993, James et al. 1998, Mayall 1991). There are a number of ways for researchers to tap into children's repertoires for acting and interacting. The local ASPRO2 teams used warm-up activities as part of the introductory procedure; some added dramatization and role-playing using toys and dolls for some parts of the focus group. The Tenerife team (Canary Islands, Spain) decided to be more daring and explore a game-playing context for the entire focus group, primarily for the younger children. The procedures for the games are described in this chapter, followed by some observations about their utility and outcome.

Games in Focus Groups

Focus group moderators strive to promote a relaxed atmosphere in which participants feel secure to express their opinions and attitudes freely, and interact with each other much more often than with the moderator. Ideally, the moderator fades into the background as the discussion progresses and, thus, is able to participate in "structured eavesdropping" (Powney 1988). When "productive" conversation between children fails to materialize, moderators may be tempted to retreat to a "partisan stance" (Denscombe 1995), attributing the vacuum in discussion to a dislike of the focal issue or the result of children's resistance tactics (e.g., mischief, peer rivalry). Jokes, anecdotes and side arguments – sources of rich information in focus groups (Kitzinger 1995:299) – presuppose that the participants are so fully engrossed in the task at hand that moderators are peripheral or simply another participant. The creation of an absorbing and stimulating child-centered "immersion" event is a – if not <u>the</u> – major challenge for moderators, and the use of games contributes to this effort.

Game techniques help the participants to focus on each other rather than on the moderator. Using games in focus groups is not new. Clue-based "parlour games" (charades, treasure hunts, missing object or person searches) and projective techniques (word-association, sentence-completion tasks) are often used in market research focus groups, along with cartoons or pictures to initiate group story-telling (Stewart & Shamdasani 1990:90). Dramatizations of narratives enrich focus group interaction (Albrecht et al 1993:61). Through creating group stories about fantasy themes and dramatizing group narratives, participants discover shared views or construct a mutual reality (Bormann 1982:291).

Game materials can assist with keeping a task in focus; for example, participants can be instructed to arrange a set of cards containing statements into categories, to create taxonomies, and present and defend their rationale to the group (Kitzinger 1995). The final lay-out of the cards is less important than the process of supporting opinions or reaching a consensus. Using the cards diverts the concentration of the participants away from not only the moderator (as a power figure or central player), but away from each participant's self-conscious attempts to "interact" and on task at hand – the playing of the game. This is precisely the goal of implementing game-centred focus groups with children.

In 1996, when the Tenerife team began to formulate a game-playing approach for its focus groups, there were few examples of similar strategies from the scientific literature. The suggestion that "stimulus materials might be warranted" for children's groups (Steward & Shamdasani 1990:99) seems to imply that children need something extra to help them participate (and for adults, additional stimuli are not particularly "warranted"). This notion is reminiscent of classical models of childhood socialization which situate children as apprentice adults. In contrast, current anthropological and sociological approaches to childhood view children as agents who should be studied in their own right, independent of adult-defined trajectories (see, for example, James, Jenks and Prout 1998). The Tenerife team decided that children might need a different kind of focus group environment where the stimulus materials were embedded in a game. The games created for the local study were not used as a way to prompt children to act like adults, but to give them a sense of freedom to "be" children. By the time the team had finished its exploration, other studies had also initiated new innovative approaches with groups of children and youth; for example, Frankland and Bloor introduced the idea of "focusing materials" (1999:145).

Using focus groups with children helps to discover the way in which they tell stories, rather than to search for "validity" or "Truth" from the content (Green 1997). Strangely enough, the question of truth in adult focus groups is rarely brought up as a methodological issue, as if it is assumed that adults tell the truth – or at least can distinguish between fantasy and reality in their narratives. If the emphasis is on the ways in which children develop narratives and act them out, rather than on the content the stories produce or the questions they successfully answer from the moderator's check list, then the issue of truth becomes less relevant. In this line of reasoning, the use of games in focus groups is an invitation for the participants to explore "responses" on their own terms and from within their own boundaries. Structuring focus groups around games and play is a step in the direction of new explorations and innovations.

Focus Group Games for ASPRO2

The warm-up and fantasy games developed for ASPRO2 were based on an interest in gaining access to children's knowledge and understandings about asthma. The main objective of all of the games was to promote interaction between the children focused on their ways of living with asthma. Some of the games might be classified as simply "contexts promoting play" in the sense that "play" is more of a spontaneous "happening" than a structured "game". These types of theoretical clarifications are beyond the scope of the essentially descriptive vignettes which follow.

Warm-up games

The need for a warm-up period before the focus discussion formally begins is suggested in almost all focus group how-to manuals. Adults are often left to their own devices; most of them have a repertoire of strategies for interaction to rely on when they find themselves in a group of strangers. Children have their own strategies as well – some of them go unnoticed by adults. Other tactics, such as pouting, sulking, bullying, or withdrawing may become all too noticeable, even from the first moments of the focus group encounter.

During ASPRO2 project-level planning sessions, it was decided to purposely pull the children into possibilities for interaction with each other, rather than to leave them to their own methods of making friends in a new environment. There was an appreciation for the observation that it is usually difficult for children (or even adults) to sit around a table and "say a few words" about themselves to strangers. Some may be so concerned about introducing themselves that they do not listen to how the others identify themselves; thus, at the end of the "round-robin" no one seated at the round table remembers very much about the others. Warm-up games need to be non-competitive, while drawing out the personal characteristics of the children. They are designed to use the skills and information that most school-aged children can easily access. Thus, almost all of the local studies included (or had ready "just in case") at least one simple warm-up game in their protocol, usually the "ball-toss" – which the Tenerife team elaborated upon with small variations.

<u>Variations on the ball-toss</u>

In its simplest version, a category of "identity" information was decided on for each round of tossing the ball between all of the children <u>and</u> moderators – name, age, number of siblings, school name. Additional rounds provide extra warm-up (e.g., when the children seem too reserved or not relaxed with the situation) by selecting categories asking for more personal information such as the name of a favourite video game, television show, hobby, teacher, friend, and so on. A more complicated version allows the person holding the ball to change the category; i.e., each time the ball is tossed, a different category can be named, chosen by the thrower. This allows for the children to verbalize curiosities about each other; they can ask questions which, under other circumstances might be considered "prying" or even "rude". They can also direct questions to the moderator by simply tossing the ball in her/his direction.

The "Spider's Web"

This game uses a ball of thick yarn or medium weight twine to create a spider's web which results as the ball is tossed between the children and the moderators. After forming a circle and agreeing with the rules of the game, the first player states her/his name and tosses the ball to the second player, making sure to hold on tightly to the end of the yarn. The next player to catch the ball states her/his name and the name of the preceding player, and finds a part of the unraveled yarn to hold onto before tossing the ball to the next player. A wide variety of response categories can be added to add more strands to the web, thereby engaging (and entangling) the children to a greater extent; e.g., colours, age, teacher's name.

Making name tags

Children can be given self-stick labels (or cards with a safety pin) and coloured pencils (or felt-tipped markers), and allowed time to make their own name tag – which is also useful for the moderators in conducting the discussion. One variation uses labels with a small figure in the corner, each with a connection to asthma; e.g., inhaler, pill bottle, furry animal, flowers, feathers and pillows. The procedure can be expanded by asking the children to explain their choice or preference for a selecting a particular label.

Drawing pictures

Drawing pictures in a group can promote interaction among children; e.g., questions between children about what each will draw, small comments during the process, verbalizations and sound effects which they attribute to the figures in their drawings. The Tenerife team preceded some of its focus groups by asking the children to draw a picture of the last time they "didn't feel well", a procedure used in qualitative studies of children's perceptions of illness (Sachs 1990, Trakas 1990, Trakas & Sanz 1992, 1996, Bush et al. 1996). They needed about fifteen minutes for the task, followed by a chance to explain their drawing to the group, an activity which was audio recorded to supplement the analysis of the focus groups.

Fantasy games

A large proportion of most children's play consists of engaging in fantasy games where they assume the roles of real and imaginary characters and create scenarios with other children and sometimes adults. This "natural" play of children was used as a basis for developing the interactive games for the focus groups conducted in Tenerife. The role playing and fantasy game motifs are described below.

The "Game of the World"

The "World Game" is an enlarged table game with a 2.5 by 1.5 meter game board. The players are invited to take a trip around the world using their (oversized) marker-piece to indicate their progress around the board. Placing the game board on the floor allows the children to move around and be ready to organize the performances which are specified during the game. The board, designed and painted by the local research team, consists of a series of squares connected in rows and curves drawn on a background of depictions of various places in the world. Players take their turn by tossing the dice and, according to the number shown, move their marker-piece forward towards the end square. The game is over when all of the players have completed their trips around the world and returned "home".

Some of the squares have instructions for the player to draw an "activity card" or a "question card" from the game board. Moving the marker-piece forward on the board depends on answering the question or performing the designated activity. The question cards refer directly to the themes in the moderator's format; for example, "What do you do to prevent an asthma crisis?" or "Name some asthma "triggers"? The other members of the group discuss the answer according to its "correctness" or "completeness"; if necessary, moderators help with reaching a consensus. The activity cards invite the children to develop a scenario and play a role in the resulting skit; e.g., "Pretend that you are a father and need to buy asthma medicines from the pharmacy for your child", "Pretend you are a mother who is taking care of her child with an asthma crisis", Pretend that you are a television announcer and you must tell the audience about asthma." Sometimes the activity cards designate that other members of the group (including the moderator) need to be involved in the skit; further, children have the freedom to invite others in the group to participate in their skit, scenario or task.

"Continue the Story"

This activity is designed to help children create a collective narrative about familiar (or not) objects, events and experience related to asthma. The objects, events and related figures are depicted on set of cards – about the size of playing cards or a little larger in order to allow for a clear identification of the intended content of the drawing. The content is based on the everyday life of children with moderate to severe asthma; for example, using an inhaler, taking a pill, avoiding asthma "triggers". Other activities are also included such as swimming, reading, resting in bed, dancing – which carry a variety of meanings for children with asthma; e.g., for some children, swimming is not a usual activity; for others, laying in bed is rare (except when sleeping). The figure on each card symbolized the beginning of a story; the game is played by children continuing the story.

The cards are placed face down (figure-side down) and the top card is turned over. Each child takes a turn to explain what is happening in the figure or sketch. A timer with a bell is used so that all the children have about the same amount of time to add to the continuing story. The moderators can also take turns, sometimes using their time to redirect the story and bring it back into focus when children wandered off the subject.

Role playing with props

This game uses two types of materials: 1) a set of cards, each with a name for various characters – mother, father, physician, teacher, pharmacist, child without asthma, best friend, etc. 2) a set of props, actual objects which can be interpreted to symbolize (or not) each of the categories printed on the cards, such as a string of pearls and a handbag for the mother, a hat and briefcase for the father, a stethoscope for the physician, and so forth.

The cards are placed with the name of the role facing down and each child selects a card at random; the one selected designates the "role" that each child will play in the skit or scenario. The props are distributed to assist in supporting the role that each child will play and remind the participants (and moderator) about the identity of each player. The "plot" of the scenario can be decided upon by the children or selected (and directed by) one of the moderators. After discussing general ideas for the "script", the play begins.

Since the game was still in the experimental stage, the Tenerife team decided to leave the selection of the scenario plot and its direction to one of the moderators to avoid having to manage too many unknowns. The general outline for the scenario was usually the following: A child with asthma, played by the moderator, is taken for a visit to the doctor, played by one of the children. Following the consultation, the parents (played by the children) go to the pharmacy to fill the prescription for asthma medication and/or visit the child's teacher to explain the problem.

"Surprise Bag"

Stories can also be developed around small items, relative to the subject of the focus group, placed in a surprise bag. For the purposes of the ASPRO2 focus groups, the bag contained items such as a peak-flow meter, an inhaler, direction flyers from medicine boxes, small furry toy animals, artificial flowers, etc. The children are gathered around the bag – the larger, the better – and take turns reaching into the bag, pulling out an object at random, and explaining what it is or represents. The other children are encouraged to follow-up with their interpretation(s) or tell a story about the object.

A game of chance with oversized dice

This game is organized around the same goals as the "surprise bag" – to create a story about an object. A set of oversized dice, large enough to allow for clear depictions of real objects on each side, was made from heavy cardboard. Each child took a turn to toss the dice and attempted to develop a story about the figures which appeared on the top sides. The game can be expanded with additional dice using questions and scenario suggestions printed or pictorially depicted on the sides.

Creating a TV advertisement

The children in focus groups were asked to prepare a TV advertisement on "the positive and good aspects of having asthma". In a short planning session (5-10 minutes), the children devised a "script" and then presented it for the "television" – the video camera. The negotiations in selecting the topic, the ideas to be presented, and the ways to present them are as important as the presentation of the final product, the advertisement or the "TV spot".

Evaluating the Focus-Group-as-Game Approach

Generally two types of game-playing approaches are used in focus groups: One uses games to initiate certain phases in the process (i.e., warm-up games, specific "focusing materials); the other structures the entire focus around playing a game. Games as introductory activities have been used in adult focus groups and formed part of the ASPRO2 focus group protocol. The second approach, game-playing as the centre and essentially the "entire" focus group is new to the repertoire. Although the initial reservations about using this approach proved largely unfounded, it is important to review them here as a means to concur (or not) on its validity. Four viewpoints are examined, paralleling the issues which were raised and discussed in ASPRO2 coordination meetings.

- Child-centred evaluations
- Perspectives of the game planners
- Weighing the practical pros and cons
- Methodological strengths and weaknesses

Child-centred evaluations

It would be easy to conclude, from the perspective of children, that creating a focus group around playing a game cannot fail to please them and will have only a positive effect on all the participants and the total undertaking. Viewing the video tapes of the focus groups organized around games strongly supports a picture of all of the children intensely engaged with each other and collectively focused on the goals as outlined in the original list of themes. In each group, all of the children, without exception, participated by acting out a role and voicing an opinion. The moderators, in contrast to their central place in the introductory phases of the focus group, appear in the games and role-playing mainly when invited by the children to participate – to help with materials, to take the role of a player in a skit or perform in some way that is initiated by the children.

The games that held the most interest for the children were those with an end goal, such as the "world game" – which also includes ample opportunities for moving around the large game board, changing positions on the floor, standing up and walking about, and so forth. The role-playing activities provided impression information about how children with asthma experience relationships with other ("non-asthmatic") children, and how they describe interactions with peers related to the management of their condition ("crises", avoiding "asthma triggers", attempts at concealment or "normalization"). The games which asked children to explain or demonstrate the use of concrete objects, such as those in the surprise bag or depicted on the faces of the dice, were successful in stimulating the expression of opinions and knowledge – which were often countered, tenaciously defended, and sometimes ended in arguments. The task of creating and presenting a television advertisement served as a good tactic for the introducing of video taping the focus groups. The children were eager to be "on stage", often competing with each other to place themselves in front of the "television" (i.e., the video camera). If they had any "adult inhibitions" about being filmed, the children did not reveal them.

In spite of the success of these focus groups as games, it would be a mistake to view this approach as the answer to the "problem" of engaging children in interactive focus groups or to assume that all children (or all groups of children) will respond as enthusiastically as did the children in Tenerife. Not all children like to participate in games, particularly when adults are present, obviously observing them and video-taping them. Older children are less likely to welcome game focus groups, just as adults are not particularly enthusiastic about playing warm-up games.

Perspectives of the game planners

The idea for creating focus groups around games was inspired by the concerns of young educators when they observed that the initial groups (piloting) did not seem to involve very much interaction. They decided that the younger children were boxed in by the original format and that a radically different approach would be necessary in order to enable the children to interact with each other. Their evaluation concentrated mainly on the quality of interaction produced by the game(s) and agreed that, particularly for the younger children, their approach was more effective than the formal, conventional format. They concluded that the interactions were "real" rather than "contrived" and even though the skit was "pretend", the essential content was not "fantasy" but based on their real-life experiences and understandings.

The moderators were pleased to observe that as each game progressed, the children seemed to be increasingly more absorbed by the game, less concerned about the presence of adults in the focus group, and that they were allowed to assume a peripheral position to the activity created by the children. For example, when a activity card in the "World Game" directed a child to improvise an interaction between a pharmacist and parent, the child asked, "Who is going to be the pharmacist? The other children pointed to the assistant moderator – "Here's the person for that! Right here!!" The assistant moderator abandoned making observational notes and joined the game.

Weighing the practical pros and cons

At the project level, concerns were voiced about the possibility that the game-playing atmosphere of the focus group would have a negative effect on the order of things; that the situation might get out of hand. For example, the moderator's capabilities to keep the objectives of the focus group in perspective would be challenged, or that the children's enthusiasm for the game would tempt them into hyperactivity and overly energetic physical contacts with each other (e.g., jostling, bumping). To the contrary, the more engrossed and satisfied the children became with the game, the less the moderator needed to intervene with "disciplinary" measures.

Some of the sessions were video recorded which initially required some thought about how to camouflage several adults within a small group of children. Not only were two adults involved, one the moderator and the other the assistant (passive, observational), but a third adult was also present -- the one operating the video camera. Sometimes there were four children and three adults, in a situation where the adult-child hegemony was already an inherent feature of children's focus groups. This "imbalance" did not interfere with the children's game-playing or their development of role-playing activities; indeed, sometimes the children tried to bring the camera operator into the games. During the "make an advertisement" activity the video camera was, of course, part of the skit; it was the television camera representing the audience.

Methodological strengths and weaknesses

At least three project-level methodological questions were asked:

- Does the approach compromise the integrity of the themes in the focus group format?
- Are game focus groups methodologically still focus groups, or are they another type of technique; e.g., "play groups"?
- Is the approach consistent with the contemporary theories of childhood which guided the development of the project protocol?

Since this was a concerted action involving set of shared objectives and methods between all the participating research units, there was concern that the game itself would become the focus and that the carefully planned format would be abandoned. In fact, a preliminary analysis of the data indicates that the themes outlined in the ASPRO2 format and moderator's guide were addressed during the games – at least as fully, or more, as in more formal and traditional focus group styles.

In general, the question of whether the approach used in Tenerife could still be considered as part of the focus group genre is a matter of perspective. Methodological purists may argue that by organizing an entire focus group around a game (not only the warm-up phase) significantly changes the key characteristics of the "original" technique; thus, the event cannot be considered as a focus group. Researchers, who hold a more dynamic perspective on qualitative methods, may insist that the focus group concept is expected to and must evolve. In the end, there is nothing sacred about the focus group label; if the scientific community objects to retaining the title of focus group when referring to the approach used in Tenerife, another label can be devised. There are more important issues to be considered such as how the game approach conforms with and complements the contemporary perspectives on childhood from anthropology and qualitative sociology.

Adult verbal interaction involves prototypes of what is "proper"; what can be said and in what way. Children's communication also has its protocol; some topics are discussed with peers but are avoided when adults enter the scene, or the discussion between children is impeded by too many adults hovering over them. The focus group as a game-playing event allows the children to construct the happening and direct the moderator to hear their voices (compared a more standard protocol which elicits a question-answer session, but not a focus group). A nice example is provided by an 8 year-old boy whose "Game of the World" activity card instructed him to have a (pretend) prescription filled for asthma medicines. He described all sorts of asthma medicines, their chemical actions on the body, and their brand names to the "pharmacist" (the assistant moderator) who remarked:

> Whew! That is a lot of information. Where did you learn about all of that? [the boy] From my brother. He's in medical school. But, hey! Wait a minute --- I'm not a university student - I'm only a first-grader!!

This example shows that children can be good "reporters" and good potential candidates for complying with medical prescriptions. In focus groups they are, as other observers note, good historians and story-tellers (Ireland & Holloway 1996). It also shows how children, within the context of focus group games, are able to separate themselves from the "game" and re-address "reality". The latter point is central to preparation of children's focus groups – which should not be presumed to "behave" as adult focus groups.

Games always have a set of rules; young children are fond of game rules -- as well as of changing the rules to suit them. The way that children maneuver to change game rules reveals the wide range of strategies that children employ in order to claim, proclaim and justify themselves as social actors. Conducting focus groups within the framework of a game diminishes the moderator-children distance and avoids the necessity for moderators to indulge in standard focus group introductories such as, “We are interested to hear what you will tell us”, “You don’t have to raise your hand to talk” (e.g., see Menacker et al. 1999). Even though these comments are honestly expressed and intended to help the children to feel at ease, they may ask themselves “How am I supposed to talk with this adult, or talk with the other kids in front of an adult? Why should I?” With a game, all the children know that they will have the chance to play; hence, they will automatically be given their turn to speak and state their opinions. They can be enabled to act …

References

Albrecht TL, Johnson GM and Walther JB 1993. Understanding communication processes in focus groups. In: *Successful Focus Groups: Advancing the state of the art* (A Sage Focus Edition), DL Morgan (ed). Sage, London.

Bormann EG 1982. Fantasy and rhetorical vision: Ten years later. *Quarterly Journal of Speech* 68:288-305.

Bush PJ, Trakas DJ, Sanz E, Wirsing R, Vaskilampi T, Prout A (eds) 1996. *Children, Medicines and Culture*. Haworth Press, New York.

Christensen P and James A (eds) 2000. *Research with Children: Perspectives and practices*. Falmer Press, London.

Denscombe M 1995. Explorations in group interviews: An evaluation of a reflexive and partisan approach. *British Educational Research Journal* 21:131-148.

Frankland J and Bloor M 1999. Some issues arising in the systematic analysis of focus group materials. In: *Developing Focus Group Research: Politics, theory and practice*, Sage Publications, London.

Green J 1997. Risk and the construction of social identity: Children’s talk about accidents. *Sociology of Health and Illness* 19(4):457-479.

Ireland L and Holloway I 1996 Qualitative health research with children. *Children and Society* 10:10-12.

James A 1993. *Childhood Identities: Self and social relationships in the experience of the child.* Edinburgh University Press, Edinburgh.

James A, Jenks C, Prout A (eds) 1998. *Theorizing Childhood.* Polity Press.

Kitzinger J 1995. Introducing focus groups. *British Medical Journal* 311:299-302.

Mayall B 1999. *Children, Health and the Social Order* Open University Press, Buckingham.

Menacker F, Aramburuzabala P, Minian N, Bush P J, Bibace R 1999.Children and medicines: What they want to know and how they want to learn. *Journal of Social and Administrative Pharmacy*, 18(1): 38-52.

Powney J 1988. Structured eavesdropping. Research Intelligence -- *Journal of the British Educational Research Foundation* 28: 10-12.

Sachs L 1992. Sweet medicine: Swedish children's perceptions of illness and medicine. In: *Studying Childhood and Medicine Use*, DJ Trakas and E Sanz (eds). ZHTA Medical Publications, Athens.

Stewart DW and Shamdasani PN 1990. *Focus Groups: Theory and practice.* Sage (Applied Social Research Methods Series), London and Newbury Park.

Trakas DJ 1992. Heavy and light illnesses – and good medicines: Accounts from Greek children. In: *Studying Childhood and Medicine Use*, DJ Trakas and E Sanz (eds). ZHTA Medical Publications, Athens.

Trakas DJ and Sanz EJ 1996. *Childhood and Medicine Use in Cross-Cultural Perspective.* European Union, Luxembourg.

Capturing Moments and Movement

Analyzing focus group interaction and dynamics

Deanna J Trakas

Focus groups may be viewed as events composed of layered verbal and non-verbal behaviours occurring within a matrix of multi-dimensional interactive dynamics. This type of statement tends to contribute to the mystique of focus groups; nevertheless, they do seem to have a life of their own (Albrecht et al. 1993:51). They are often unpredictable performances involving players, usually strangers, acting out a variety of momentary relationships to each other. The script produced in a focus group is likely to be very different from a text created from an interpersonal interview. The analysis of the materials (e.g., audio and video tapes, sociograms, dialogues, texts) generated by focus groups requires an exploration of the potentials and boundaries of qualitative data management techniques, most of which were developed primarily for use with individual interviews. To challenge the idea that focus group analysis is "basically the same as analysing any other qualitative self-reported data" (Kitzinger 1995:302), it would be quite appropriate to argue in favour of *focus group specific* approaches to analysis and interpretation.

The range of analytical approaches to focus group materials includes suggestions to "consider the words" and "find the big ideas" (Krueger 1994:149-151) or to explore the use of socio-linguistic theory (Myers and Macnaghten 1999) and computer-generated schematics for describing verbal content (Stewart and Shamdasani 1990). However, there is clearly much more than verbal interaction taking place in focus groups and the "kernel" of their analysis is not necessarily to be found in the words spoken during sessions (Myers and Macnaghten 1999). This is particularly true for the analysis of children's interaction in focus groups and an over-reliance on thematic content may result in the loss of important and challenging information; for example, contexts of emotion such as outbursts of hilarity, nervous laughter, reactions to anger or jealousy.

Conducting focus groups with children challenges researchers to re-examine many of the major issues in qualitative research methodologies. As reviewed in previous chapters, modifications in (adult) focus group protocols are useful in accommodating the needs of children. It seems logical that the analytical directions and strategies would require similar child-centred adjustments. This conforms with new trends in focus group analysis in general, which place attention on the participatory process (Baker and Hinton 1999) and collective agency (Callaghan 2005), the influence of context (Green and Hart 1999) and dynamics of interaction (Kitzinger 1994), and use interpretative approaches (Frankland and Bloor 1999) to decode the way meanings emerge as well as catalogue bits of data (e.g., see Catterall and Maclaren 1997).

This chapter addresses some of the practical and analytical issues related to interactions, dynamics and "data management" observed, continually addressed and, to some extent, problematized by the members of the *Living with Asthma in Childhood* project (ASPRO2):

- Preparing session materials for analysis; transcripts, worksheets, coding
- First level analysis; working with the script, context, holistic overviews
- Interpreting children's focus groups; examples, levels of analysis
- Cross-cultural considerations; language, threats to quality

Sorting Through the Data

Qualitative researchers usually maintain large archives of textual materials accumulated during their research; journals, observational notes, transcripts of interviews, content analysis charts. In the past, most ethnographers sorted through their fieldwork data by hand, usually finding software programmes for qualitative data management and analysis cumbersome. Currently, virtually all focus group manuals recommend audio taping and transcribing the entire discussion along with suggestions for the use of computer software programmes for textual and contextual analysis. Portable recording instruments and computer supported systems of data management assist in creating the image of an objective data base which includes all the minute details of each comment and interaction in a focus group.

It is problematic to assume that less impressionistic interpretations or more objective conclusions will result when the hand-written notations of moderators are scrutinized by software packages for content analysis. In general, the discourse on "objectivity" in qualitative research – in fact, in quantitative projects and positivist science – is far too lengthy and "hi-tech" to examine here. Instead, a few suggestions to preserve the quality of the data and to keep it accessible to all members of a research team are presented below. To begin with, textual analysis software should be used with a clear understanding that these programmes do not actually analyze, they *facilitate* (Frankland and Bloor 1999:147), and "... expecting these packages to do the analysis is like expecting a food processor to cook you a meal, whereas what it really does is replace your paring knife" (Morgan 1993:240). Software programmes can be useful for coding pieces of data but may require some sophisticated manoeuvres to decode constructions of meaning, or, to use the metaphors of Catterall and Maclaren (1997), the challenge is in moving beyond the snapshot to the moving picture. Even with the use of computer age technology, "truth" is often in the eye of the beholder -- or, the ear of the listener.

Transcription of audio tapes

In the 1940s when Merton and his colleagues (Merton and Kendall 1946, Merton, Fiske and Kendall 1956) introduced the concept of "focused group interviews", hand-held audio recorders were not available. Later, when market researchers began to use focus groups, audio tapes were introduced mainly to ensure quality control and debrief the moderators (Frankland and Bloor 1999:144). As with personal interviews, group discussions are often transcribed in preparation for content analysis. However, "unless a systematic approach of some kind (be it analytic induction or some other system) is undertaken, then it is difficult to see the advantages of audio-transcription" (Frankland and Bloor 1999:154).

Transcribing audio text into visual text takes considerable time and it could be questioned whether it should be done at all or if independent transcribers should be paid so that moderators could concentrate on conducting additional focus groups and analyzing transcripts and videoed sessions. Nevertheless, the activity of transcribing constitutes a form of re-entry to the experience, provides immediate feedback for the moderators, and actually marks the beginning of the analysis. Logically, moderators should be directly involved in the transcription of audiotapes (Frankland and Bloor 1999:146), a process which enhances the accuracy of the transcripts (Knodel 1993). While moderators may feel relieved when they do not need to do the transcribing themselves, they lose the "hands-on" experience. They miss out on the opportunity to review their lived experience groups and to see how the series of sessions which they moderated unfold, "gel" and solidify.

In the process of transcribing it is important to preserve the idioms of children's "talk" and to avoid correcting their grammar and syntax. When transcribing the ASPRO2 groups, special attention was given to identifying and linking the speakers with their comments in order to strengthen the contextual placement of discussion; e.g., the "procession" of individual children during the interaction as they took turns in speaking, contradicted ideas and changed opinions. Transcripts also included notations about non-verbal behaviours such as smiles and frowns between participants, nodding the head to indicate an answer or making a face (grimacing) to show disagreement. Independent transcribers will not be able to make these parenthetical remarks, another reason why moderators should do their own transcriptions.

Focus group worksheets

Writing field notes during focus groups, a task usually assigned to the assistant moderator who is responsible for tasks related to keeping order, also contributes to the quality of the data (Morgan 1993). In ASPRO2, notations were included as a routine and central part of the focus group worksheet, which was also used for listing technical information such as the names of the children, their ages and gender, research numbers, and code numbers of audio tapes corresponding to the session. Categories for observational commentary were also recorded on the worksheet; e.g., non-verbal interactions, pre-existing friendships between the children, indicators to identify which child speaks at which point in the discussion. As soon as possible following the session, the two moderators reviewed their preliminary impressions about the content and added their comments to the worksheet.

The worksheet is a valuable aid to transcribing the audio tape. Some verbalizations on the tape may be inaudible to the transcriber due to background noise or mumbled chatter. When several children are all speaking at once, it is difficult to ascertain which child said what. The worksheet should contain information about these overlaps in voices and can help to identify each speaker, which is important for contextual analysis. Working with the transcript and adding information to the worksheet, or vice versa, based on the moderator's memory of the session and re-listening to tracks on the audio tape helps to ensure that the transcription is as complete as possible. A holistic overview of each session can be developed by cross-checking all the sub-sets of data; e.g., the questions of the moderator, the verbal communication of each child, the children's discussion and non-verbal interaction. Other aspects of the worksheet are discussed by Hallia and Vaskilampi, this volume.

Reliability and verifiable analysis

The worksheet together with the transcript provides a record which can be reviewed by an independent researcher to assess issues such as reliability (Knodel 1993:50) and verifiable analysis; e.g., an impartial researcher should be able to code the same transcript in the same way, or a second researcher should be able to arrive at the same conclusions (Krueger 1993:78). It might be remarked that these concerns about replicability in coding are imported from positivist, qualitative research models. For qualitative researchers, at least for those who participated in ASPRO2, the requisites of reliability and verification are not necessarily of paramount importance. It is quite acceptable or even desirable when researchers, independently analyzing the data, arrive at different interpretations.

In most local ASPRO2 studies, the worksheet-transcript sets functioned as a form of quality control, particularly when the focus groups were conducted by different pairs of moderators or when the study coordinator was not involved in the data collection. The sets are more than a tool to settle issues of, for example, inter-moderator reliability; they provide a forum where different interpretations of the "same" phenomena can be explored. By working through the preparation of these two sets of data, the researchers are able to develop an in-depth familiarity with the raw data and are intellectually much better prepared to apply the intricacies of content analysis, develop holistic overviews of each group, and compare the groups to each other. Further, the reason for transcribing and the degree to which audio text is transformed to visual text (entire, segments) is not dependent on policing the validity or reliability of what transforms during a focus group.

The need to "justify" interpretation through measuring (or in some way evaluating) inter-researcher reliability which has crept into qualitative methodologies seems to be an artifact of the notion that "real" research is eventually quantitative research. Agreement in the interpretations between independent scientists observing the same "data" is valued in quantitative studies; indeed, the goal of the novice researcher is to arrive at, deductively, the same results as a more experienced colleague. In contrast, the mature qualitative scientist will get more from the data inductively, the interpretation will be richer, and probably different from that of the less experienced researcher. In this context, inter-researcher reliability recedes from a place of central importance and becomes a peripheral concern. Depending on the goals of the research and the type of analysis of focus group content planned, the entire transcription of each group may not be necessary; i.e., preparing for focus group analysis is not only about transcriptions. A moderator's worksheet of the type used in ASPRO2 can be used interactively with segments of group narratives and enhance the contextualization of specific portions of the interactions (and individual narrations) in the session.

Writing, Reading and Analyzing Focus Group Scripts

By the time focus group worksheets and transcriptions are completed, the researchers usually have developed a good picture of the content of their focus groups and the direction that their analysis will take. One approach to content analysis begins with the identification of topics and issues which are coded or "indexed" (Frankland and Bloor 1999:145) by key words or letter-number combinations. At a later stage of analysis thematic "clusters" are defined and assigned relationships with each other through "code mapping". Unlike interpersonal interviews, focus groups involve a number of actors; thus, it is acceptable to speak of "coding the script" (Kitzinger 1995:302) or, even, "writing the scenario". Even though the script has already been acted out in the focus group and is objectively portrayed in the transcript, the drama needs to be "located". While coding helps to determine how much useful data there are for interpretations (Morgan 1993), "useful data" are not necessarily determined by bulk; important interpretations may rest on moments of hesitation or silence.

Using the moderator guide

Coding is an inductive enterprise; it is impossible to predict all the possible index references which need to be devised. The moderator guide can be used for the initial set of codes (Knodel 1993). However, using the moderator guide as starting point for coding may lead to building a tautology; i.e., the themes "found" in the transcript match those in the guide so perfectly that the search for other issues may be truncated – and nothing new is discovered. Thus, the relationship between the moderator's guide and qualitative analytic tactics is problematic: While the guide is necessary to conduct the sessions, it might be best set aside afterwards, particularly when analysis begins.

Ideally, coding the content of focus groups will not follow a previously constructed script, but will apply principles from grounded theory (Charmaz 1990,

Glaser and Strauss 1976, Strauss and Corbin 1990). New codes for content and "flags" for leading or biased questions will be introduced, and transcripts which were previously read and coded will be re-read to see if the newly coded themes and issues also appear in these earlier transcripts. Coding is a cyclical process, referring back and forth between transcripts, and indexing is "essentially inductive in nature, with categories emerging from the analyst's hermeneutic absorption in the text ... the process is not reductive; the data are retained in richness and context, but comparative analysis is facilitated" (Frankland and Bloor 1999:146).

Content, context, interaction

Content analysis provides answers to questions about what children say, but it might not provide insight about *why* they say what they say – or avoid mentioning. It may not be particularly helpful in arriving at "deeper" levels of meaning. Without a systematic exploration of the context in which the issues and opinions arose in the first place, thematic analysis can become an exercise in futility. This point is also stressed in the adult focus group literature, but it is even more critical in children's groups (see Vega and Aramburuzabala, this volume) – where it is tempting to impose conclusions based on adult "reality". In the absence of an analytical description of the context, the content of interaction may be misunderstood and interpretations become superficial.

Group interaction is the element which separates a focus group from an individual or group interview; therefore, interactions of all sorts must be analyzed as pieces of data. The moderators explicitly exploit group dynamics and "analyze the resultant interactions as productions of data" (Wilson 1997:211). Clearly there is much more happening in focus groups than simply the exchange of verbal messages; coding the script can enrich the indexing of topics by adding codes for special types of narratives; e.g., jokes, argument, censorship, change of opinion, deference, boredom, emotion. Problematic areas should also be flagged; e.g., lines in transcripts which may have resulted from children's compliance or discomfort with the moderator, being overwhelmed by a majority opinion, or feeling bullied.

Inter-subjectivity is an ingredient in all forms of interaction, independent of age, and should be included as an analytical perspective. Initially – or until recently – inter-subjectivity usually referred to the interaction of non-human actors; used to describe pre-cultural interactions. The application of this version of the concept to children's focus group materials should not be misconstrued as an indication that children are "little savages", that their interactions are somehow more guided by nature than culture and other methodologically naïve, uninformed assumptions.

Visualizing the actors

Group responses are influenced by factors such as compliance, identification and internalization (Albrecht et al. 1993:61-64), which, in turn are played out in various social settings. The identification of the roles that the participants play can form the basis for analyzing the group dynamics. One starting point could be the behaviours of the various actors noted on the transcript or worksheet; e.g., the relevant person, the irrelevant participant, the humorous one, the leader, the follower, the loner. Visual methods of organizing the actors can also be used; for example, Venn diagrams, sociograms, flow charts, and grids.

The deviant-case approach (Kitzinger 1994, Frankland and Bloor 1999:151) is useful in analyzing the way in which minority opinions are presented and responded to by the participants. However, in focus groups, it is not always clear if interruption, silence, or unfinished sentences are signs of deviance or an artifact produced by the interaction (Frankland and Bloor 1999:153). Low levels of trust between the participants or with the moderator may result in the communication of what is perceived as socially desirable information at the expense of socially undesirable information (Albrecht et al. 1998:63). Thus, only a partial picture emerges, particularly when ethics and moralities are involved (for example, with most illnesses) or when perceived inequalities are present (such as might be the case with children and adults).

What Kitzinger and Farquhar (1999) refer to as "sensitive moments" in focus groups may have "interactional impact" and should be identified and considered as part of the interactional analysis. Honesty (or dishonesty) may be one of the issues which characterizes a sensitive moment, but data should not be classified in terms of honesty—dishonesty or truth—falsehood (Kitzinger 1994). Because pretence is often a central element in focus groups and children enjoy playing the game of pretend (see Anderson, this volume), the issue of honesty – or rather, the Truth – might best be avoided when evaluating children's groups. In general, for all focus groups, moderators might want to stay away from the temptation to use "triangulation" to ferret out participants who are not "telling the truth". The rather extreme example of using a "focus meter" in adult focus groups to measure galvanic skin response to identify untruthful participants and to "get deeper inside their head" (Morgan 1993:240) is not expected to provide much insight for honest moderators interested in discovering the meanings of sensitive moments.

Writing holistic overviews of individual focus groups

The group dimension of the process of the sessions has often been overlooked in analysis, a point which several researchers raised early on (Carey 1994, Carey and Smith 1994, Green and Hart 1999, Kitzinger 1994, Wilkinsen 1998). In fact, this is one of the continuing concerns up to the present time (Darbyshire et al. 2005, Hayden & Budow 2003, Webb and Kevern 2001). Developing overviews about individual focus groups brings together the transcript-worksheet data sets, coded mapping or scripts, and moderator reflections. Writing holistic essays about each group may be more productive for researchers interested in interpretative approaches than searching for key phrases and conducting content analysis. They may purposely decide to avoid the approach of excerpting segments of group discussions and assigning codes, preferring to study the "meaning" of the group in its entirety.

For researchers committed to visual representations of their data, a "grid" format can be used to compare focus groups (Knodel 1999:47-49). The strategy can supplement the holistic essay approach or be embellished as a matrix representation. It begins with placing the group identifier (number, letter) on one axis followed by plotting selected variables on the other axis; e.g., age, gender, range of opinions, level of interaction between participants. The cells on the grid contain key phrases or brief summaries related to the variable; e.g., peer group or age range, same or mixed gender, compliant or diverse opinions, silent or highly interactive.

Interpreting Children's Focus Groups

Interpreting qualitative data is an inductive process which depends on the ability of the researcher to work through many levels of materials. How is it possible "...to separate the disparate layers of respondents' explanations and meanings from the researchers' interpretations?" (Wilson 1997:212). To what extent are the stories told in children's focus groups "tailored" for an adult audience (Green and Hart 1999)? Who is the interpreter – the children who provide their opinions and explanations, or the moderator? Rather than avoid these questions, researchers need to identify themselves as the interpreters, be aware of their predisposing assumptions, be willing to examine their biases and to allow validity to the children's voices – as they would with adults.

Thematic categories

Both individualized interviews and focus groups are directed discussions and it is "natural" to search for thematic (or content) categories, and see which "fit" with the direction of the discussion. Interviews and focus groups unfold under different circumstances with implications for selecting the approaches for their analysis. Interviews represent personal stories disclosed in privacy, created with and for the interviewer. Stories can be analyzed by using thematic categories to assist in making comparisons and by identifying similarities and differences.

In contrast, the stories developed and presented in focus groups are a result of a much more public process; personal stories are revealed to a larger audience. It may be a methodological mistake to rely entirely on thematic content categories to analyze individual stories with the intent of relating them to the other individual voices in the group. The extant prevailing method in focus group analysis is the use of content categories; but this approach may produces simply "shopping lists"; for example, lists of opinions, sources of information, children's citations of asthma triggers, metaphors for the body and symptoms. This is an adequate approach if identifying levels of "knowledge" is the goal of the research, as with health education studies; but putting the elements of these lists together to locate meaning (conceptualizations, valuations, desirability, etc.) takes more time and it is unclear if lists of this type are the place to begin in this pursuit.

Conceptual categories

Interpretation is facilitated by indexing transcripts with concept-rich categories which define the properties of an event according to when it arises, how it changes, its consequences, and relates it to other conceptual categories (Charmaz 1990:1168). This approach, central in the application of grounded theory, extends basic content analysis of interviews to a wider phenomenological level. For example, a reference to "pain" can be heard as a word intended to convey a certain content, but it can also operate as a concept. As a *content* category it is an easy marker to locate when the word or its synonyms and metaphors are mentioned; e.g., discomfort, "ouch", feeling "out of sorts". As a *conceptual* category, pain is more difficult to locate in the script; it is not always a linguistic reference point, it extends beyond acute physical sensations to feelings of social, psychological and spiritual dysphoria (Trakas 1998).

Ways to work with the topic and concept of pain in children's focus groups about asthma might include the following:

- Select excerpts which specify pain or its synonyms; bodily discomfort, fear, anxiety, apprehension about when the sensation or feeling will stop, etc.

- Review the script to locate the context for discussions about pain; e.g., Does the group bring up the subject collectively and all participants enter into the discussion? Is there one person who is speaking alone when other participants seem to be interested in other topics? Is the issue of pain discussed only when the moderator asks about it?

- Identify forms of discourse about pain; e.g., agreement with others (or not); joking formats; argumentative structures; comparison narratives about intensity and effect.

- Locate moralizing dialogues (or monologues) about pain; e.g., it has no purpose; it is a form of punishment; it is a result of not following rules or a form of punishment; it is something that can be remedied; it "teaches" the person about specific matters such as avoiding allergy triggers as well as providing lessons about more general existential issues (enjoyment, understanding, etc.)

- Place the speakers in relation to each other and explore the contexts of the single voices; e.g. other subjects discussed during the same focus group, taboo topics, favourite complaints.

First and second level interpretations

First level interpretations are usually based on thematic categories and code groups. These are essentially ethnographic descriptions and interpretations of the researcher without theoretical integration. Examples of first level interpretations from ASPRO2 include children's needs for asthma information; ideas about asthma causes and prevention; attitudes about specific medicines; feelings of social isolation associated with having been diagnosed with the condition.

Second level interpretations begin with using the data to develop new hypotheses and usually require a fresh look at the data. At this level interpretations about the applied potentials of focus groups might be explored; for example, using them in educational interventions, assessing changes in participants' attitudes following the session (children and parents often felt better after participating in an discussion about asthma). Theory-building is part of this level; for example, formulating new theoretical perspectives about how children interact in focus groups, analyzing the impact of the context or "style" on the data, or comparing focus groups on a cross-cultural basis – which might have become Part II of this book. .

Cross-Cultural Considerations

When children's focus groups take place in several research sites, a number of issues arise not only about the "standardization" of the protocol and its implementation, but about the implications for comparative analyses. How feasible is multi-sited qualitative research – with focus group studies as a particular approach which, in one culture or with homogeneous participants, can be problematic? This section takes up two of the many difficult matters which are relevant to qualitative research conducted in different cultures: language and content analysis.

Language

It is helpful if a small, select number of focus group transcriptions can be exchanged between research teams, each using their own local language in the collection of data. The question is: In what language can it be exchanged? Since English was the operating language for ASPRO2 meetings, it was used for the translated transcripts. Each team provided English transcripts of one to three of their focus groups and distributed them to other members of the project. By exchanging unanalyzed data, the project members had the chance to formulate preliminary strategies for potentially comparative ways to approach analysis; for example, locating basic categories for content analysis, flow charts or sociograms to describe group dynamics.

While the richness of the original language modalities, such as children's idioms of expression or metaphors for their asthma symptoms and medication might be altered in translation, there are advantages to being willing to engage in the challenge. The process may serve to reveal the idioms and metaphors which might have been otherwise taken for granted by the researchers. It is not unusual for indigenous terms and phrases to assume new meaning when they are explained to a non-native speaker. In fact, this is precisely what happened in ASPRO2, resulting in a different awareness about the familiar and how to convey it to the "other". It forces each researcher to ask questions about the spoken word; for example, "How would I translate the expression into another language without losing the meaning?" This way of working also addresses concerns about individual researcher subjectivity and helps to anticipate issues that arise in multidisciplinary and inter-cultural research.

Standardizing codes

Since the project was multi-lingual, considerable time was devoted to the consideration of how to manage categories of data for comparison between local studies. Similar discussions had taken place in two previous multi-sited projects – predecessors to ASPRO2 – and most of its members were more than familiar with the debates that went on during coordination meetings about how to manage and compare data between and across research locations. The pros and cons of developing an extensive code book to classify descriptive information from interviews with children were reviewed from the experiences of the project members in previous concerted actions. For example, the "cook book" which resulted from an earlier project had served as the foundation for a data bank where all indexed data (in code numbers) from all teams could be entered and made available to all participants, regardless of their operating language (see Bush et al. 1996).

This precise system, already tested in a large undertaking, could have been accessed and improved upon for the content analysis of the focus groups; but this was not to be the case. The advantages of the standardized project-level coding system were eventually outweighed by practical and methodological disadvantages. Thematic and especially conceptual categories are relative to cultural meanings; therefore they differ considerably between cultures. Assigning codes to categories and indexing is sensitive enough work as it is, without adding (or imposing) the cross-cultural element. Further, most of the members of the research team had also participated in the project, notorious for its cookbook, and were well aware of the difficulties in trying to develop a uniform coding package. Indeed, the activity of coding threatened to become an end in and of itself. As Krueger (1993) emphasizes, quality can be compromised if too much time is spent on one level of analysis – in this case, attempting to set up and use standardized coding for categories of talk and behaviour in a number of different cultural settings.

Objectivity and Reflexivity

Science and objectivity are so nearly synonymous in the minds of most observers that research which does not substantiate a sense of objectivity, does not stand up as scientific – its data are "soft", its analysis lacks rigour, and its conclusions little more than philosophy. Even so, in the human and life sciences there is a growing appreciation of the idea that there is no crime in the lack of objectivity. In this view, biased interpretations are inescapable; the error lies in neglecting the search for and critical examination of the source of the bias. Qualitative research requires reflexivity, particularly when the research has an ethnographic character and the scientist becomes, in a very real sense, the data collection instrument. In the process of data analysis, all possible interpretations are sought out and valuable; thus (in contrast to quantitative research), it is not alarming when two different moderators arrive at two different conclusions. In fact, it is desirable – quite a different view from quantitative research where these differences might be explained by flaws in the study design or a failure in reliability. Such differences offer opportunities to explore researcher-centred mechanisms which contribute to the variations in interpretations or conclusions.

Even though focus groups are contrived situations, they can be viewed as ethnographic events (see Anderson, this volume); if they cannot (or should not) be analyzed as such, there is no reason to avoid using ethnographic techniques in analysis. In fact, focus groups offer abundant opportunities for participant observations – the main technique of ethnographic research. To continue, developing holistic descriptions of focus groups requires the skills which ethnographers cultivate in their writing. Although ethnographers traditionally work alone (save for field assistants who often accompany them – and sometimes spouses, partners, significant others and children), many recognize the advantages of conducting fieldwork in pairs (e.g., ethnographer – physician, ethnographer – junior scientist). Thus, the moderator dyad encourages creating reflexivity between the moderators; cross-checking observations, discussing body language, and in general moving within the realm of intersubjectivity which is important in the ethnographic enterprise. These components need to be openly examined rather than avoided according to an iconoclastic decision that focus groups "are not and never will be" ethnography.

The analysis of focus groups in the 1990s was a bit of a mystery to novice moderators and other researchers involved in harvesting and processing information produced. Part of the reason is located in the early how-to focus group manuals which are weighted with details about planning and performing the sessions, with limited equivalent thought about analysis. The literature of the time promoted the assumption that data from focus groups could be handled by using any number of already existing analytical approaches from qualitative research. Content and narrative analyses were the most often cited techniques; however, in the absence of details, it appeared that they were used mainly to identify themes from the discussion across groups, rather than analyze the groups internally as entities or events.

The issues which preoccupied the members of ASPRO2 parallel those which appeared in the focus group literature of the 1990s. In addition, we were under the illusion throughout most of the project that the technique is tightly-bounded and governed by strict rules which define it. We projected what might happen if the boundaries or the rules would be bent – either in data collection or in analysis, and imagined that the focus group would cease to be such and become something else – a game-playing group or ... even worse, an un-focused group discussion. Our rigidity as neophytes interfered with being able to see that focus groups can serve different purposes; consequently, analysis should conform to the trajectory of the goals of the research rather than insist on the purity of analytical procedures. One single type of analysis cannot be imposed; indeed, not all focus group research needs to be findings-directed. The purpose of using focus groups is not only (or always) to "get" results or "produce" findings, a matter which is discussed in the final chapter.

References

Albrecht TL, Johnson GM and Walther JB 1993. Understanding communication processes in focus groups. In: *Successful Focus Groups: Advancing the state of the art* (A Sage Focus Edition), DL Morgan (ed). Sage, London.

Baker R and Hinton R 1999. Do focus groups facilitate meaningful participation in social research? In: *Developing Focus Group Research: Politics, Theory and practice*, RS Barbour and J Kitzinger (eds). Sage, London.

Bush PJ, Trakas DJ, Sanz EJ, Wirsing RL, Vaskilampi T, Prout A 1996. *Children, Medicine and Culture*. Pharmaceutical Products Press / Haworth, Binghamton New York.

Callaghan G 2005. Accessing habitus: Relating structure and agency through focus group research. Sociological Research Online 10(3).
www.socresonline.org.uk/10/3/callahan.html]

Carey MA 1994. The group effect in focus groups: Planning, implementing and interpreting focus group research. In: *Critical Issues in Qualitative Research Methods*, JM Morse (ed). Sage, London.

Carey MA and Smith MW 1994. Capturing the group effect in focus groups: A special concern in analysis. *Qualitative Health Research* 4(1):123-127.

Charmaz K 1990. 'Discovering' Chronic Illness: Using Grounded Theory, *Social Science and Medicine* 50(11): 1161-1172.

Darbyshire P, MacDougall C and Schiller W 2005. Multiple methods in qualitative research with children: More insight or just more? *Qualitative Research* 5(4):417-436.

Frankland J and Bloor M 1999. Some issues arising in the systematic analysis of focus group materials. In: *Developing Focus Group Research: Politics, Theory and practice*, RS Barbour and J Kitzinger (eds). Sage, London.

Glaser BG and Strauss AL 1967. *The Discovery of Grounded Theory: Strategies for qualitative research*. Aldine de Gruyter, Hawthorne, New York.

Green L and Hart J 1999. The impact of context on data. In: *Developing Focus Group Research: Politics, Theory and practice*, RS Barbour and J Kitzinger (eds). Sage, London.

Hyden L-C and Bulow PH 2003. Who's talking: Drawing conclusions from focus groups – some methodological considerations. *International Journal of Social Research Methodology* 6(4):305-321.

Kitzinger J 1994. The methodology of focus groups: the importance of interaction between participants. *Sociology of Health and Illness* 16(1):103-121.

Kitzinger J 1995. Introducing focus groups. *British Medical Journal* 311:299-302.

Kitzinger J and Farquhar C 1999. The analytical potential of "sensitive moments" in focus group discussions. In: *Developing Focus Group Research: Politics, Theory and practice*, RS Barbour and J Kitzinger (eds). Sage, London.

Knodel J 1993. The design and analysis of focus group studies: A practical approach. In: *Successful Focus Groups: Advancing the state of the art* (A Sage Focus Edition), DL Morgan (ed). Sage, London.

Krueger RA 1993. Quality control in focus group research. In: *Successful Focus Groups: Advancing the state of the art* (A Sage Focus Edition), DL Morgan (ed). Sage, London.

Krueger RA 1994. *Focus Groups: A Practical Guide for Applied Research*. Sage, Thousand Oaks.

Merton RK and Kendall PL 1946. The focused interview. *The American Journal of Sociology* 51:541-557.

Merton RK, Fiske M and Kendall PL 1956. *The Focused Interview:* A manual of problems and procedures. The Free Press, Glencoe Illinois. [re-published in 1990 by New York: Free Press and London: Collier Macmillan]

Morgan DL 1993 Future directions for focus groups. In: In: *Successful Focus Groups: Advancing the state of the art* (A Sage Focus Edition), DL Morgan (ed). Sage, London.

Myers G and Macnaghten P 1994. Can focus groups be analysed as talk? In: *Developing Focus Group Research: Politics, Theory and practice*, RS Barbour and J Kitzinger (eds). Sage, London.

Stewart DW and Shamdanasi PN 1990. *Focus Groups: Theory and Practice*. Sage (Applied Social Research Methods Series), London.

Strauss A and Corbin J 1990. *Basics of Qualitative Research: Grounded theory procedures and techniques*. Sage, Newbury Park.

Trakas DJ 1998. The construction of pain in childhood: Is there a place for children's voices? In: *Identities in Pain*, J Frykman, N Seremetakis, S Ewert. (eds). Nordic Academic Press, Lund Sweden..

Webb C & Kevern J 2001. Focus groups as a research method: a critique of some aspects of their use in nursing research. *Journal of Advanced Nursing* 33(6)798-805.

Wilkinsen S 1998. Focus groups in health research: Exploring the meanings of health and illness. *Journal of Health Psychology* 3(3):329-348.

Wilson V 1997. Focus groups: a useful tool for educational research. *British Educational Research Journal* 23(2) (1997):204-244.

Moving Forward
Focus groups in new terrains

Deanna J Trakas

Focus group research provides excellent examples of how the socio-historical context serves and moves the scientific enterprise – and the reverse. One of the fascinating aspects of a social history of focus groups is the way in which their image has been shaped by political and economic forces and the way research has responded to their prestige. The attractiveness and mystique of focus groups has survived for some 60 years. Moving them into the terrain of childhood in the 1990s raised several issues which, in focus group research with adults, had gone unnoticed or become "normalized"; the more obvious and practical of these were selected for development in the chapters of this book. This final chapter reviews some of new (and renewed) perspectives which have surfaced in recent focus group discourse. As with other qualitative research methods, focus groups are used by a wide variety of scientists – each finding a different utility, application and even philosophy.

A biography of focus group discussions might begin with the observation that their formative years were passed in a fairly stable, secure, homogeneous environment. Their lineage can be traced to group-interview techniques, such as those popular with sociologists in the mid-1920s (Borgadus 1926). The sociologist Robert K Merton is usually credited with being the "father of the focus group" with Paul Lazerfeld as the godfather figure in the story. In the 1940s, Lazerfeld had been commissioned by the United States Office of Facts and Figures (eventually named the Office of War Information) to organize a study about the response of the American public to war morale programmes broadcast on the radio. He recruited Merton, who organized the project using focus group discussion procedures for essentially the first time (Merton and Kendall 1946, Merton and Lazerfeld 1950, Merton et al. 1956). From the start, the focus group was given a public persona, a social reputation as a research technique which was initially created "primarily as a means of increasing military morale" (Krueger 1994:7). Apparently even Merton was ambivalent about the career of focus groups; it is rumoured that "long after he had helped devise the methodology [he] deplored its abuse and misuse" (Kaufman 2003).

The home territory of focus groups in their early years was largely confined to private sector market research in the United States where the participants were mainly adult white middle-class consumers (Krueger 1994:vii, x). Elsewhere in the behavioural sciences, focus groups appeared to be in a period of latency. Being left to lie dormant was perhaps related to the association of their roots with government military spending – a good reason for most politically conscious social scientists of the 1960s to leave them out of their methodological repertoire. At the same time, focus groups became so thoroughly embraced by market research that, for outsiders, the method and the field of marketing were synonymous. Social scientists of the time did not (yet) tend to see their respondents or informants as consumers. Even so, the notion of the "group" is so central to the human sciences, that the attraction of focus groups as a methodological approach is obvious. Even if there is a sense of the contrived, the formation of ad hoc and transient groups has become a way of life in post-modern society; self-help groups, chat groups, therapy groups, study groups … and the focus group is simply one more.

A New Era in Focus Group Research

In the late 1980s, a series of how-to manuals re-introduced the focus group *discussion* to the social sciences (Krueger 1988, Morgan 1988, Morgan and Spanish 1984, Stewart and Shamdasani 1990). Thus began an era of the "resurgence of interest" in focus groups (Lunt and Livingston 1996) and the "reclaiming of the focus group method by social science" (Chiu and Knight 1999). Discussion is part of the democratic process – and, as Krueger (1994: 238-9) informs us, focus groups are a natural part of this process: People have "hunger to be heard"; people all over the country need to talk; leaders need to listen; decision-makers need information. Focus groups are presented as egalitarian by nature – an important part of the image to be built upon in the 2000s in response to the changing times. Creating discussion – egalitarian, spontaneous, "authentic" – is one of the most crucial points in the development of methodologies for children's focus groups. What has been learned from children's groups has applicability to sessions with focus groups with "new" untried social collectivities and communities such as minorities, migrants, the elderly and other categories of persons based on, for example, medical diagnosis.

The "neglected Cinderella of social science" (Barbour and Kitzinger 1999: 200) – the focus group – became the debutante of the decade via a series of focus group publications in the 1990s (Dawson et al. 1993, Fern 2001, Kitzinger 1994, 1995); many of which were second editions of handbooks which first appeared in the mid-1980s (Greenbaum 1998, Krueger 1994, Morgan 1993, Morgan and Krueger 1997). It appeared that developments in focus group research were so rapid that the manuals required equally rapid updates for the lucrative focus group publication market. The Cinderella story was assisted by publicity which promoted focus groups as a quick and inexpensive way to produce data. This contention became unfounded rumour after focus groups took hold in the social sciences – and even if it was true for market focus groups, which give a quick turn over from implementation to findings (Vaughn et al. 1996), qualitative researchers usually prefer to have time to "work with" their data and are usually less concerned with the rapid presentation of findings.

By the late 1980s, focus groups even caught the imagination of the general public in the United States where at least 700 rooms were reported to have been designed for focus discussion research (Goldman and MacDonald 1987). Focus groups in action could be glimpsed in movie plots about the intrigues of US big business and were referred to in clever one-liners such as "Did you ever have an idea that you didn't get from a focus group?" One of the many political cartoonists satirizing the pervasiveness of the focus group depicted two animal-skin clad "cavemen" trying to navigate a square "wheel" carved from rock, while a third commented, "I don't know. Maybe we should run it by a focus group first"[1]. In the comedy film *Daddy Day Care*, the actor Eddie Murphy declares that "what we need is a focus group!" in order to find out what the children want from his day care centre. In the next scene, a group of charming, articulate and insistent toddlers are seen asking for "food for our minds" and arguing with each other about whether dolphins are fish.

The popularization of focus groups is not always considered as a positive phenomenon; in fact, the very idea that the technique had risen so rapidly in popularity was viewed with suspicion by critical social commentators. At least one member of the US press referred to focus groups in less than polite terms, as *that* research technique which "politicians, their handlers, marketeers and hucksters now find indispensable". (Kaufman 2003). Similar uneasiness was aroused by focus groups when they were introduced in Great Britain in the mid-1990s. The public rhetoric about the dangers of focus groups in the country is scathingly (but humorously) documented by Rosaline Barbour and Jenny Kitzinger (1999) in the opening paragraph of their groundbreaking edited collection about the politics, theory and practice of focus groups. Reservations about the history, reputation and political potentials of focus groups were voiced by the coordinators and researchers of the *Living with Asthma in Childhood* project (ASPRO2), but the concentration on smoothing out the practicalities of using focus groups with children was so immediate that these considerations took a back seat.

New Focus Group Terrains

To return to the chronology of the life history of focus groups, the idea of using the technique for research about the clinic – the utilization of medical care and health services – was a challenge which could not be ignored by, for example, medical sociologists and professional nurses. Beginning in the early 1990s nursing journals emerged as a forerunner in publications about focus group research in health care (Kingry et al. 1990, Murphy et al. 1992). Shortly thereafter, *Qualitative Health Research* devoted an entire 1995 issue to the presentation of focus group research in clinical and health-related settings (edited by MA Carey). Professional nursing continues to be a major promoter of focus group research (Goodman and Evans 2006, Khadka et al. 2008, Parsons and Greenwood 2000, Webb and Kevern 2001), which is probably not by chance given its patient-centred (rather than disease-centred) approach to care.

It is not surprising that the market focus group could be moved so seamlessly into the health care research setting. Up to this point, the reputation of focus groups rested mainly on research with consumers – and it did not take much imagination to see users of health care services as consumers. The notion of a "consumer of heath" conceptually organizes the clinic *as if* it constitutes a market, in the tradition of a free, competitive agora. In this perspective the "consumer of health services" is a superficial category which serves the interests of capitalist political economy (e.g., see Grace 1991); or expedites the analysis of the mechanisms of biopower and biopolitics. Nevertheless, the tendency to view patients and sufferers as consumers of health services probably contributed to the easy transfer of focus groups from the one terrain to the other, but which did little to challenge their underlying assumptions and principles in their new territory.

The success of focus groups in qualitative health research, potentially involving painful or at least emotionally-charged sessions, suggested that they might be used in studies of "sensitive populations" (Kitzinger 1994) or research about "sensitive topics" (Hoppe et al. 1995, Farquhar with Das 1999). Surprisingly (or maybe not, given the momentum of focus groups at the time), by the mid-1990s children had been engaged in focus group discussions about issues such as sexual content on television (Kaiser Family Foundation and Children Now 1996) and preteen girls were asked to talk about their concerns about puberty (Doswell and Vandestienne 1996). Focus groups with children were examined for their possible use as a resource in sexual abuse prevention (Charlesworth and Rodwell 1997) and as an event where youth could talk about living with a mentally ill parent (Garley et al. 1997) or suicide prevention (Coggan and Patterson 1998). In less than 10 years other delicate topics were added and there seemed to be very little that could *not* be considered as a focus for discussions with children and youth: Their emotional difficulties (Nevada DCFS 2002), the effects on their lives of having a father in jail (L.I.F.E. 2002), their evaluations of school-based support groups to help live with substance-addicted parents (Gance-Cleveland 2004) and their problems related to gender and violence (Snyder 2005).

Focus groups about sensitivities, feelings and emotions have the potential to contribute methodological and ethical re-alignments to the protocol. Their planners could possibly succumb to the temptation of data-driven procedures. Independently of whether focus groups are assigned to everyday situations or extreme-case scenarios (e.g., sensitive topics), it is important to allow the framework to move ahead by keeping the large picture in mind rather than stagnating in details. This is a project which requires not only consciousness, but also a certain sense of *self*-consciousness, both in the application of "modifications" as well as in a fundamental recognition of some of the underlying, contextual issues with focus groups. Self-conscious – because moving into new neighbourhoods, new social collectivities – often quite different from the researcher's personal and scientific experience, is almost by definition, uneasy, uncomfortable and stressful. And qualitative researchers already experience some degree of unease when working with children (e.g., see Descombe 1995, Hood et al. 1996.); that is, with using children as respondents, subjects, participants and informants.

By the mid-1990s, children had clearly emerged as a new social collectivity on the focus group scene. A handful of somewhat disparate examples – in terms of topic, location and the scientific training of the researchers – included the work of Green and Hart on children's assessment of risk and accidents in Great Britain (1998, 1999); Vaughn and her colleagues in Great Britain (1996); Menacker and her group on children's attitudes about medicines in the United States

(1999); Baker and her team on street children in Nepal (1996). Rachael Baker's project in Nepal is one of the very few focus group studies to have been conducted by social scientists in a non-western society during the 1990s. This alone is indicative of the confinement of the focus group to its "own backyard" – comfortable, but not particularly challenging. Other focus group projects with children in this same time frame were conducted mainly in western societies – or pertained to research with children in groups within the sociocultural parameters of the western world (Davis 2001, Horner 2000, Hill et al. 2004, Hoppe et al 1995, Mitchell 1999).

Research about children and childhood in general moved into a period when it could begin to apply the efforts of the re-theorizing which had begun in the late 1980s. Studies were no longer only on or about children, but with them (Darbyshire 2000). Research on children's health had become a million-dollar enterprise (Darbyshire et al. 2005), and focus groups were not going to be left out of the enterprise (Kennedy et al. 2001). Group discussions with children took up topics such as their perceived needs for health care (Hill 1999), their views of paediatric care (Heary and Hennessy 2002, Hennessy and Heary 2005), their ideas about health education needs (e.g., Hämeen-Anttila 2006, Hämeen-Anttila et al. 2006, Menacker et al. 1999 O'Dea 2003). It is unclear whether the resemblance between children and other health consumers is intended in these projects. A series of articles began to give attention to the methodological issues of working with children in discussion groups (focus or otherwise) (Darbyshire et al. 2005, Gibson 2007, Hurley 1998) and their perceptions on the research methods used with them (Hill 2006). Last but by no means least, the work of Myfanwy Morgan and her colleagues (2002), based on their participation in ASPRO2, is among the forerunners in the methodological evaluation of focus groups with children.

Lessons from Focus Groups with Children

This is an appropriate point to ask, what are the lessons from children's focus groups: Which issues are reaching resolution, which questions remain, and which answers are still embryonic and under construction? The focus group "kit" of the 1990s could not be taken at face value and applied to the ASPRO2 undertaking. Every possible contingency had to be considered; all possible case scenarios needed to be mapped out – some which never actually happened (but other unexpected ones did). Following the preliminary analysis of the first focus groups, the directions of the project began to unfold; even so, every small innovation needed to be weighed in terms of the entire effort – and it is precisely here that the advantages of a multidisciplinary team became evident. As a result the dialogue between different scientific disciplines, the protocol recommendations have firmed up on such matters as the ideal number of participants, guidelines for the age and gender mix, selection of focus group locations and settings, recruitment precautions, the use of warm-up activities and methods for maintaining live records of the event.

One area which remains controversial is that of "homogeneity", a matter which is usually addressed on three levels: selection of participants, the implementation of sessions, and the distance between moderators and participants. The idea that there should be some sort of homogeneity between participants is a message which is usually picked up by focus group organizers. The issue of homogeneity is exacerbated with children's groups: Age and gender need to be delicately balanced in sessions. Age differences of one or two years between participants may result in a communication impasse; or, imagine a group of seven year-olds, with only one little boy (or the reverse). It would seem simple enough to plan the synthesis of focus groups to resemble the choices of the participants in their everyday social life – unless the object of the project is to study diversity or conflict resolution.

There seem to be (at least) two ways of conceptualizing this issue. One sees diversity in and between groups as risky because it is difficult to gauge the effects of "differences in environmental and personal factors among the samples" and "the possible influence of the facilitator on the children" (Hämeen-Anttila et al. 2006:177). This perspective would support more systematic research about the characteristics of the participants and focus group outcomes; for example, the "quality of responses" (see Fern 1982). A series of studies hint that cultural diversity, language differences, and ethnic affiliations of the participants (and moderator) have an impact on their behaviour (Stanfield 1994, Watkins-Mathys 2006, and see a review article by Halcomb et al. 2007). On the other hand, most qualitative researchers are less concerned about controlling the "samples" for the purposes of comparisons (in fact, they do not usually think of focus group participants as part of a sample). Instead, they are more interested in the interactive dimensions of focus groups, for example, their performative characteristics.

Role playing and games have become an accepted and even encouraged part of academic focus groups, and stimulus materials are considered to be essential, indeed a bonus. There is nothing intrinsic about adding game-playing which compromises the integrity of the methodological boundaries of focus groups (or other qualitative methods, see for example Punch 2002). However, researchers who endorse games in sessions may hesitate to extend the strategy to using games as the entire focus group itself. There may be a concern about the "bulk" of the game interfering with the goals of the study or obscuring its research questions. Furthermore, a wide spectrum of focus group motifs, ranging from game-dominated to discussion-centred, reduces the persuasive power of comparisons of content, interactions and findings. This is not a question of "Validity" or "Truth"; simply a recognition that different circumstances can provide different data – both valid, both true – but not necessarily within the demands of these concepts as they are used in quantitative methodology.

The debate about how much play is too much – which dominated several ASPRO2 coordination meetings – may mask deeper methodological questions. A continual and subtle friction can be detected in the discourse about the use of quantitative and/or qualitative approaches in the evaluation of specific strategies for focus groups planned around different "types" of participants. Thus, the cloudy area is more about compatibility and comparability between sessions than whether focus groups organized around a game are deviations from their original concept as *discussion*-based activities; i.e., sitting down and talking. It is usually assumed that a similarity between the background of the moderators and participants facilitates this process. Focus groups are very different from group interviews where the researcher is in the *centre* of the circle (real or imaginary), directing the questions to the respondents. In contrast, the focus group moderator facilitates the interaction *between* the participants and their movement among the different "points" in the circle.

Synthesizing focus group performances hinges on the ability of the moderator to set the boundaries and maintain the framework for dialogues of interactions. When the moderators are professionals already trained in working with a particular age group or social collectivity (e.g., the elderly, children, migrants, gays, street people), conflicts of interest may arise. For example, primary school teachers might seem to be the logical choice for moderating children's focus groups – they know children, understand childhood, have capabilities in maintaining order. However, in the role of moderator, they may not be able to let go of those capacities valued in the classroom (and by colleagues) … but not, perhaps, useful in a focus group. Physicians may find it quite impossible to relinquish their status as providers of health care and medical information; stepping into the role of a moderator in the focus group which is, ideally, an egalitarian event may seem to be simply out of the question.

With their roots in white middle-class America, focus groups did not move very far from their geographic origins until the late 1990s; most studies were conducted in the United States, Great Britain and Australia, where, for the most part, moderators and participants were linguistically and culturally similar. By the early 21st century, this picture had changed: Focus groups were used in a health research project with rural adolescents in South Africa (Onya and Fisher 2004), in discussions with young people about AIDS/HIV prevention in Zimbabwe (Gandidze et al. 1993), and AIDS/HIV risk assessment with men from Japan (Kawaguchi et al. 2002). Some projects were market focus group studies which went beyond the scope of consumer opinions to show how focus groups in Ethiopia about telecommunication technology were used to supplement quantitative information (Woldekidan and Lishan 2005) or by raising questions about cultural and linguistic differences among the participants in sessions in China (Watkins-Mathys 2006).

New questions about the "problem" of diversity and focus groups arose; this time about differences between moderators, participants and the context of the research. Moderators taking focus groups into new territories were instructed to "become familiar" with the geographic, political, economic, and sociocultural background of the area and its population (Vissandjee et al. 2002:826). Experiences in "other cultures" – even though they were sometimes in the same geopolitical country – contributed to an awareness on the part of focus group researchers about how racial and ethnic identity determines what is seen and how it is seen (Ahmed 1993, Stanfield 1994). Conducting focus groups in culturally diverse or "ethnic" terrains involves more than the mastery the local language (see also Fallon and Brown 2002, Halcomb et al. 2007). Participants may complain about the condescending behaviour of their bilingual moderator (Yelland and Gifford 1995) or comment about the "white girl in a sari" who tried to "trick" them into revealing private opinions (Stanfield 1994:108). These kinds of possibilities were also present in children's focus groups where the participants could be suspicious of their moderators who "go native" with the over-use (or mis-use) of youthful jargon or mis-appropriated apparel.

Indeed, focus groups seemed to be less complicated in their early years, when homogeneity was the rule rather than the exception; when the contemplation of the "effects" of cultural differences between moderators and participants received less attention. Apparently the more varied the actors in focus groups are, the more researchers become concerned about honesty, transparency, truth – which eventually leads to discourses on objectivity and subjectivity. Researchers planning to conduct focus groups with children usually begin with questions about children's capacity to tell the truth or to distinguish between fact and fantasy. Even seasoned moderators may fix their strategies on a preoccupation with locating honest answers among the complexities of children's psychosocial development, their vulnerability to peer pressure, desire to please the moderator, and so on. The issue of honesty, and particularly fantasy, is rarely raised in reference to adult focus groups – although concerns about fact and fantasy, truth and honest, are expected to surface when focus groups are moved up the age ladder to include the elderly.

Balances – Participation, Power, Social Inclusion, Solidarity

The quest for truth in the form of proof and evidence-based research is part of the legacy of the "belief" in objectivity on which positivist science prides itself. The issue for qualitative research is not "objectivity", but subjectivity – and particularly, intersubjectivity; for example, how an interview becomes the creation of two people interacting, or how a focus group becomes the engagement of several people pursuing the exposition of a task outlined for them by the moderator. Qualitative researchers tend to look at narratives and dialogues as representations of "reality" which are constructed in response to personal and contextual factors; for example, the need to tell a story in a particular way, the desire to convey unpleasant emotions to the moderator who may be seen as a source of help, attempts to please the interviewer ... to entertain the other participants. A shared *habitus* facilitates intersubjectivity between the participants and the moderator(s); obvious and deeply internalized differences are not necessarily impediments (see Callaghan 2005 on the process in adult groups).

The spread of focus groups into new social geographies and cultural terrains has introduced a series of concepts which emphasize the central role of the participants; among these are power dynamics, empowerment, participatory research and solidarity. Perhaps Krueger anticipated the ideological nature of the "globalization" of focus groups when, in 1994, he commented on the "... hunger of people ... all around this country [the US]... to be heard" (1994:239). Thus, engaging people in focus groups, particularly the disinherited, takes on the sense of a moral obligation. Focus group ethics such as those guarding recruitment, consent, privacy and public disclosure are then seen in quite a different light. From this perspective, focus groups are participant-powered; the participants have the right to create the interaction rather than allow it to be imposed upon them by the moderator(s). In this spirit, the moderator is as much a participant as researcher, thereby inviting participatory research. Focus groups have the potential to bring shared understandings to the surface and enable the participants to experience a sense of empowerment which can help them to identify solutions (O'Kane 2000).

However, as Baker and Hinton (1999) point out, focus groups should not be seen as automatically and inherently participatory research; participatory is not necessarily empowering – and equating it with empowerment may misplace "reality". They would like to see more attention given to mapping out the power hierarchies – relations of power and control which are brought into the focus group agenda and which may hinder participation and social inclusion. For example: child-adult interactions involve unequal power dynamics (Mauthner 1997, Valentine 1999); adults as professional interviewers have much greater cultural capital independent of the age of the participants; and when there is a difference in cultural capital, there is a potential for symbolic violence (Bourdieu 1999). Through discussion, shared concepts can be uncovered and "... through owning these self-defined concepts, [participants] achieve a greater understanding of their predicament (Freire 1972).

Social science research is a political activity – and it is unavoidable that it involves some form on intrusion of people's lives (Lindsay 2000:209). Focus groups may be viewed as contrived or ethnographic; artificial or natural. Ethnography itself may be more contrived than previously believed; hence, abundant references to "performance" in contemporary ethnographic writing - and focus groups may be more "natural" than we think; even children may view them as less unusual events in their everyday life than has been represented in some parts of this book. While the presence of adult moderators may signify an intrusion on children's spontaneous play, there are few domains where children interact without the presence of at least one adult (Mayall 1994). Thus, it is not surprising that they tailor parts of their stories for the adult moderators (Green and Hart 1999:24), conform to the will of the stronger participants in focus groups, and enter into contrived negotiations and artificial agreements – and other processes of agency characteristic of their *habitus* and collective identity.

Qualitative research with children sensitizes the investigators to the difficulties associated with separating ethical and methodological issues, obliging them to consider the issues of power dynamics, collective identity, decisions, negotiations – among the examples particularly visible in focus groups. Reflections about empowerment and solidarity are relative to the most recent directions of focus group potentials but more importantly, indicative the incredible capacity of focus groups to expand their list of adaptations and variations. It is unclear if identifying these altruistic characteristics is part of a larger discourse on ethics, qualitative research and field studies; or if it is part of an effort to create a new "look" for focus groups quite distant from their marketing research image. In either case, focus groups stand without extra rhetoric and their talent for flexibility is part of their charm.

Endnote

[1]Unfortunately the sources have been obscured with time; hopefully no copyright infractions have occurred. Kitzinger and Barbour, as they have their own collection of political cartoons parodying focus groups (1999:2), could probably provide the correct reference. Indeed, it is impressive to encounter colleagues who also find "focus group humour" (or graffiti) worthy of being collected and referenced. Presently, a number of internet links have archived focus group cartoons; my searches have not yet uncovered the one I cite in this chapter.

References

References

Ahmed WIU 1993. Making black people sick: 'Race' ideology and health research. In: *'Race' and Health in Contemporary Britain*, WIU Ahmed (ed). Open University Press, Buckingham.

Baker R and Hinton R 1999. Do focus groups facilitate meaningful participation in social research? In: *Developing Focus Group Research: Politics, theory and practice*, RS Barbour and J Kitzinger (eds). Sage Publications, London.

Baker R, Panter-Brick C et al. 1996. Methods used in research with children in Nepal. *Childhood* 3 (2): 171-193. [Special issue "Children out of Place", M Connolly and J Ennew (eds)]

Barbour RS and Kitzinger J 1999. Afterword. In: *Developing Focus Group Research: Politics, theory and practice*, RS Barbour and J Kitzinger (eds). Sage, London.

Bogardus ES 1926. The group interview. *Journal of Applied Sociology* 10:3472-3482.

Bourdieu P 1996. *The State Nobility: Elite schools in the field of power*. Stanford University Press, CA.

Callaghan Gill 2005. Accessing habitus: Relating structure and agency through focus group research. *Sociological Research Online* 10(3).

Carey MA (ed) 1995. Issues and applications of focus groups". *Qualitative Health Research* [Special Issue] 5(4).

Charlesworth LW and Rodwell MK 1997. Focus groups with children: A resource for sexual abuse prevention program evaluation. *Child Abuse and Neglect* 21(12):1205-1216.

Chiu L-F and Knight D 1999. How useful are focus groups for obtaining the views of minority groups? In: *Developing Focus Group Research: Politics, theory and practice*, RS Barbour and J Kitzinger (eds). Sage Publications, London.

Coggan C and Patterson P 1998. Focus groups with youth to enhance knowledge of ways to address youth suicide. In: *Suicide Prevention in the Global Context*, RJ Kosky et al. (eds). Plenum Press, New York.

Darbyshire P 2000. Guest editorial: From research on children to research with children. *Neonatal, Paediatric and Child Health Nursing* 3(1):2-3.

Darbyshire P, MacDougall C and Schiller W 2005. Multiple methods in qualitative research with children: More insight or just more? *Qualitative Research* 5(4):417-436.

Davis A 2001. Getting around: Listening to children's views. Proceedings of the Institution of Civil Engineers – *Municipal Engineer* 145(2):191-194.

Dawson S, Manderson L, Tallo VL 1993. *A Manual for the Use of Focus Groups*. Boston: International Nutrition Foundation for Developing Countries.

Denscombe M 1995: Explorations in group interviews: An evaluation of a reflexive and partisan approach. *British Educational Research Journal* 21:131-148.

Doswell WM and Vandestienne G 1996. The use of focus groups to examine pubertal concerns in preteen girls: Initial findings and implications for practice and research. *Issues in Comprehensive Pediatric Nursing* 19:103-120.

Kaiser Foundation and Children Now 1996. The family hour focus groups: Children's responses to sexual content on TV and their parents' reactions. Kaiser Foundation and Children Now, Oakland CA.
http://eric.ed.gov/ERICWebPortal/custom/portlets/recordDetails/detailmini.jsp?_nfpb=true&_&ERICExtSearch_SearchValue_0=ED409082&ERICExtSearch_SearchType_0=no&accno=ED409082

Fallon GR and Brown RB 2002. Focusing on focus groups: lessons from a research project involving a Bangladeshi community. *Qualitative Research* 2(2):195-208.

Farquhar C (with R Das) 1999. Are focus groups suitable for 'sensitive' topics? In *Developing Focus Group Research: Politics, theory and practice*, RS Barbour and J Kitzinger (eds). Sage Publications, London.

Fern EF 1982. The effects of group size, acquaintanceship and moderator on quantity and quality of responses in using focus groups for idea generation. *Marketing Research* XIX:1-13.

Fern EF 2001. *Advanced Focus Group Research.* Sage Publications, Thousand Oaks, CA.

Freire Paulo 1972. *Pedagogy of the Oppressed.* Penguin, Harmondsworth.

Gance-Cleveland B 2004. Qualitative evaluation of a school-based support group for adolescents with an addicted parent. *Nursing Research* 53(6):379-386.

Gandidze M., McGrath N, Peters A 1993, *A report on focus group discussions with out of school youth on perceptions and strategies for communicating about AIDS.* Ministry of Education and Culture, Harare Zimbabwe.

Garley D, Gallop R, Johnson N, Pipitone J 1997. Children of the mentally ill: A qualitative focus group approach. *Journal of Psychiatric and Mental Health Nursing* 4:97-103.

Gibson F 2007. Conducting focus groups with children and young people: Strategies for success. *Journal for Research in Nursing* 12:473-483.

Goldman AE and MacDonald SS 1987. *The Group Depth Interview: Principles and practice.* Prentice Hall Englewood Cliffs, New Jersey.

Goodman C and Evans C 2006. Using focus groups. In: *The Research Process in Nursing*, 5th edn, K Gerrish and C Lacey (eds). Blackwell Publishing, Oxford.

Grace VM 1991. The marketing of empowerment and the construction of the health consumer: A critique of health promotion. *International Journal of Health Services* 21(2)329-342.

Green J and Hart L 1998. Children's views of accident risk and prevention: A qualitative study. *Injury Prevention* 4:457-479.

Green J and Hart L 1999. The impact of context on data. In: *Developing Focus Group Research: Politics, theory and practice*, RS Barbour and J Kitzinger (eds). Sage, London

Greenbaum TL 1998. *The Handbook for Focus Group Research*, 2nd edn. Sage Publications, Thousand Oaks.

Halcomb EJ, Gholizadeh L, DiGiacomo M, Phillips J, Davidson PM 2007. Literature review: Considerations in undertaking focus group research with culturally and linguistically diverse groups *Journal of Clinical Nursing* 16(6):1000-1011.

Hämeen-Anttila K, Juvenen M, Ahonen R, Bush PJ, Airaksinen M 2006. How well can children understand medicine related topics? *Patient Education and Counseling* 60:171-178.

Hämeen-Anttila K 2006. Education Before Medication: Empowering children as medicine users. Doctoral Dissertation. Department of Social Pharmacy, Faculty of Pharmacy, University of Kuopio.

Heary C and Hennessy E 2002. The use of focus group interviews in pediatric health care research. *Journal of Psychology* 27(1):47.

Hennessy E and Heary C 2005. Exploring children's views through focus groups. In: *Research Children's Experience: Approaches and methods*, S Greene and D Hogan (eds). Sage Publications, London.

Hill M 1999. What's the problem? Who can help? The perspectives of children and young people on their well-being and on helping professionals. *Journal of Social Work Practice* 13(2):135-145.

Hill M 2006. Children's voices on ways of having a voice: Children's and young people's perspectives on methods used in research and consultation. *Childhood* 13:69-89.

Hill M, Davis J, Prout A, Tisdall K 2004. Moving the participation agenda forward. Children and Society 18(2):77-96.

Hood S, Kelley P, Mayall B 1996. Children as research subjects: A risky enterprise. *Children and Society* 10:117-128.

Hoppe MJ, Wells EA, Morrison DM, Gillmore MR, Wilsdon A 1995. Using focus groups to discuss sensitive topics with children. *Evaluation Review* 19(1):102-114.

Horner SD 2000. Using focus group methods with middle school children. *Research in Nursing and Health* 23:519-517.

Hurley N 1998. *Straight Talk. Working with children and young people in groups*. Joseph Rowntree Foundation, York.

Kaiser Family Foundation and Children Now 1996. The family hour focus groups: Children's responses to sexual content on TV. The Henry J Kaiser Family Foundation (with Children NOW), ERIC.
http://eric.ed.gov/ERICDocs/data/ericdocs2sql/content_storage_01/0000019b/80/16/b2/dd.pdf

Kaufman M 2003. Robert K. Merton, versatile sociologist and father of the focus group, dies at 92. The New York Times, February 24, 2003.
http://query.nytimes.com/gst/fullpage.html?res=9B04E0DB1E3DF937A15751C0A9659C8B63

Kawaguchi K, Kazama T, Kashiwazaki M, Sugawara T, Kaneko K, Suzuki K, Kimura H 2002. Some findings through focus group interview in Japanese three cities risk assessment for the AIDS prevention among gay and bisexual men in Japan. International Conference on AIDS July 7-12 Tokyo Japan.

Kennedy C, Kools S, Krueger R 2001. Methodology considerations in children's focus groups. *Nursing Research* 50(2):124-125.

Khadka J Woodhouse MJ, Margrain T, Ryan B, Davies N 2008. Focusing Children in Focus Groups. *Ophthalmic and Physiological Optics* 28(1):99.

Kingry MJ, Tiedje L, Friedman LL 1990. Focus groups: A research technique for nursing. *Nursing Research* 39(2):124-125.

Kitzinger J 1994. The methodology of focus groups: The importance of interaction between research participants. *Sociology of Health and Illness* 16(1):103-121.

Kitzinger J 1995. Introducing focus groups. *British Medical Journal* 311:199-302.

Krueger RA 1988. *Focus Groups: A practical guide for applied research.* Sage, Newbury Park, CA.

Krueger RA 1994. *Focus Groups: A practical guide for applied research, 2nd edn.*. Sage Publications, Thousand Oaks CA.

L.I.F.E. 2002. Protocol for focus groups on the Living Interactive Family Education Program's impact on the children of incarcerated fathers.
http://extension.missouri.edu/fcrp/lifeevaluation/protocol.htm

Lindsay G 2000. Researching children's perspectives: Ethical issues. In: *Researching Children's Perspectives*, A Lewis and G Lindsay (eds). Open University Press, Buckingham.

Lunt P and Livingstone S 1996. Focus groups in communication and media research. *Journal of Communication* 42:78-87.

Mauthner M 1997. Methodological aspects of collecting data from children: Lessons from three research projects. *Children and Society* 11:16-28.

Mayall B 1994. *Negotiating Health: Primary school children at home and school.* Cassell, London.

Menacker F, Aramburuzabala P, Minian N, Bush PJ and Bibace R 1999. Children and medicines: What they want to know and how they want to learn. Journal of Social and Administrative Pharmacy 16:38-52.

Merton RK and Kendall PL 1946. The focused interview. *The American Journal of Sociology* 51:541-557.

Merton RK and Lazerfeld PF 1950. Continuities in Social Research: Studies in the Scope of "The American Soldier". Free Press, Glencoe Illinois:. [story of Samuel Andrew Stouffer 1900-1960]

Merton RK, Fiske M and Kendall PL 1956. *The Focused Interview:* A manual of problems and procedures. The Free Press, Glencoe Illinois. [re-published in 1990 by New York: Free Press and London: Collier Macmillan]

Mitchell L 1999. Combining focus groups and interviews: Telling how it is; telling how it feels. In *Developing Focus Group Research: Politics, theory and practice*, RS Barbour and J Kitzinger (eds). Sage Publications, London.

Morgan DL 1988. *Focus Groups as Qualitative Research*. Sage, London.

Morgan DL (ed) 1993. *Successful Focus Groups: Advancing the state of the art*. Sage, Newbury Park CA.

Morgan DL and Krueger RA 1997. *Focus Group Kit, Vols 1-6*. Sage, London.

Morgan DL and Spanish M 1984. Focus groups: A new tool for qualitative research. *Qualitative Sociology* 7(3):253-270.

Morgan M, Gibbs S, Maxwell K, Britten N 2002. Hearing children's voices: Methodological issues in conducting focus groups with children aged 7-11 years. *Qualitative Research* 2(1):5-20.

Murphy B, Cockburn J, Murphy M 1992. Focus groups in health research. *Health Promotion Journal of Australia* 2(2):37-40.

Nevada DCFS 2002. Focus Groups Executive Summary. Nevada Division of Children and Family Services.
http://www.dcfs.state.nv.us/Reports/FocusGroupsExecutiveSummary.pdf

O'Dea JA 2003. Why do kids eat healthful food: Perceived benefits of and barriers to healthful eating and physical activity among children and adolescents. *Journal of the American Dietetic Association* 103(4):497-501.

O'Kane C 2000. The development of participatory techniques: Facilitating children's views about decisions with affect them. In: *Research with Children*, P Christensen and A James (eds). Falmer Press, London.

Onya HE and Fisher AJ 2004. Qualitative adolescent health research – focus groups: a rural South African example. *Journal of Child and Adolescent Mental Health* 16(2):117-125.

Parsons M and Greenwood J 2000. A guide to the use of focus groups in health care research: Part 1. *Contemporary Nursing* 9(2):169-180.

Punch S 2002. Interviewing strategies with young people: The secret box, a stimulus material and task-based activities. *Children and Society* 16(1):45-56.

Snyder B 2005. Video games and gender: Focus groups among elementary school children. Paper presented at the annual meeting of the American Sociological Association, Marriott Hotel, Loews Philadelphia Hotel, Philadelphia, PA, Aug 12, 2005. http://www.allacademic.com/meta/p23591_index.html

Standfield JH 1994. Ethnic modelling in qualitative research. In *Handbook of Qualitative Research*, NK Denzin and YS Lincoln (eds). Sage, London.

Stewart DW and Shamdasani PN 1990. *Focus Groups: Theory and practice*. Sage, Newbury Park CA.

Valentine G 1999. Being seen and heard? The ethical complexities of working with children and young people at home and at school. *Ethics, Place and Environment* 2(2):141-155.

Vaughn S, Schumm JS, Sinagub J 1996. *Focus Group Interviews in Education and Psychology*. Sage, Thousand Oaks CA.

Vissandjee B, Abdool N, Dupere S 2002. Focus groups in rural Gujarat, India: A modified approach. Qualitative Health Research 12(6):826-843.

Watkins-Mathys L 2006. Focus group interviewing in China: Language, culture and sense-making. *Journal of International Entrepreneurship* 4(4):209-226.

Webb C and Kevern J 2001. Focus groups as a research method: A critique of some aspects of their use in nursing research. *Journal of Advanced Nursing* 33(6):798-805.

Woldekidan K and Lishan A 2005. E-usage index focus groups survey in Ethiopia: 2005. www.researchictafrica.net/images/upload/FG_EthiopiaStandAloneReport.pdf

Yelland J and Gifford S 1995. Problems of focus group methods in cross-cultural research: A case study of beliefs about sudden infant death syndrome. *Australian Journal of Public Health* 19(3):257-263.

Notes on the Authors

Michael Anderson received his PhD in Anthropology from Hull University, UK. His dissertation on identity and bicultural children in Greece formed the basis for his ongoing research about communication between children and adults, and the development of group techniques for intergenerational research. As project consultant, Michael brought this experience and his tenacious integrity to *Living with Asthma in Childhood.* Presently he is the Section Leader for Management, Leadership and Enterprise Courses for the Lifelong Learning Network in the West Midlands (UK) and a freelance management leadership consultant.
dr.michael-anderson@talk21.com

Pilar Aramburuzabala began research about children and health behaviour when she was a member of the two concerted actions which preceded *Living with Asthma in Childhood.* She received her PhD in Educational Psychology from Complutense University, Madrid, with a dissertation on children's use and perception of medicines as a basis for health education programmes. Pilar has participated in research projects with Patricia J Bush in the USA, and was co-coordinator of the focus group with children study in Madrid. Currently she is Associate Professor in the Faculty of Psychology, IE University in Segovia, Spain.
pilar.aramburuzabala@ie.edu

Patricia J. Bush, PhD, is Professor Emerita, Georgetown University School of Medicine, Washington, DC, USA, where she directed the Division of Children's Health Promotion, Department of Family Medicine. She holds degrees from the Universities of Michigan, London, and Minnesota. As a pharmacosociologist, she has a long and ground-breaking record of research projects and over 90 publications about health behaviour and the medicine use process, particularly among children. In 2007 she was awarded the N. Sklifosovsky Medal by the

Coalition on Safe and Rational Use of Medicines (CoRSUM) in recognition of her ongoing efforts to establish global programs advocating educating children about medicines. As the focus group trainer for the initiation of the *Living with Asthma in Childhood* project, she was invaluable to the team as a resource person and consultant.
pjbushwork@comcast.net

Annette Drews graduated from the University of Amsterdam with a PhD in Medical Anthropology and teaches at the Fachbereich Sozialwesen, Hochschule Zittau/Goerlitz, Germany. Her research interests reflect a variety of places, topics and perspectives ranging from her doctoral dissertation on metaphors of pregnancy and birth in Zambia to her recent book on the spiritual power of African-inspired ritual music. Annette trained a large team of focus group moderators for the Goerlitz study during the *Living with Asthma in Childhood* project.
a.drews@hs-zigr.de

Outi Hallia was an active member of the Kuopio, Finland, team for the three consecutive concerted actions about children and their perceptions of illness and medicine. Her practical experience with children and insights about young people were central in the planning of the *Living with Asthma in Childhood* focus group format and moderator's guide. Outi is currently using her degree in Cultural Anthropology as a vocational rehabilitation counsellor with a particular interest in working with immigrants.
outi.hallia@dnainternet.net

Aspasia (Aspa) Menexiadi was the administrative assistant to the *Living with Asthma in Childhood* project coordinator. As a PhD candidate in Social Anthropology at the University of the Aegean, she was also trained to participate in all levels of the research from the planning of focus groups to their analysis. Aspa left her own fieldwork in a therapeutic community for recovering substance abusers in favour of establishing a candle shoppe in an Athens suburb – which the project members agree is in perfect keeping with her aura.

Emilio J Sanz holds an MD and a PhD in Clinical Pharmacology from the University of LaLaguna, Tenerife, the Canary Islands, and currently Dean of its Medical School where he introduced courses in medical anthropology, with an emphasis on society and pharmaceuticals. He is the co-editor of three books on the topic of childhood and medicine use resulting from the previous concerted actions. During the *Living with Asthma in Childhood* project, he was the Coordinator for Spain's participation, working with his teams in Tenerife and Ma-

drid. Presently he is finishing his second doctoral dissertation on the cultural role of pharmaceutical for a PhD in medical anthropology.
ejsanz@gmail.com

Anastasia (Tasoula)Topalidou, in spite of her youth, must be considered a veteran in the dual role of assistant to the Project Coordinator and researcher without frontiers and for all seasons. Throughout *Living with Asthma in Childhood* she managed to stay several steps ahead of the demands of the project. Currently Tasoula is using her anthropological training, organizational skills and analytical mind serving the public in the Athens Citizen's Advocate Offices.
topalidou@synigoros.gr

Deanna J Trakas conducted her dissertation fieldwork in a Greek village, went native and joined the research staff at the Institute of Child Health in Athens, from where she initiated and coordinated the concerted actions on children, illness and medicines. *Living with Asthma in Childhood* was intended to provide closure for a set of projects; instead, it opened up new methodological horizons, particularly for anthropologists. Presently, she is Associate Professor in the Department of Social Anthropology and History, University of the Aegean where she continues trying to enrich the area of medical anthropology in Greek academia.
d.trakas@sa.aegean.gr

Tuula Vaskilampi has received her Doctorate in the Social Sciences from the University of Jyväskylä, Finland and is presently Professor of Medical Sociology in the School of Public Health and Clinic Nutrition, University of Kuopio. She has been instrumental in promoting qualitative health research and active in establishing medical anthropology in Finland through her works on the social and cultural dimensions of health in modern society, including biomedicine and alternative medicine. Her research and teaching interests include the ethical aspects of prevention, spiritual health and folk medicine. She is co-editor of a book resulting from a previous concerted action on children and medicine use. Tuula was central in the development and piloting of the *Living with Asthma in Childhood* focus group protocol and was the Coordinator for Kuopio team.
Tuula.Vaskilampi@uku.fi

Maria Vega is Professor in the Department of Educational Psychology, Complutense University, Madrid, which is also the department from which she received her PhD. Her research interests include children's psychosocial developmental levels, classroom psychology and educational methods – initial and in-

service teacher training. Maria was the Co-coordinator for the Madrid study of *Living with Asthma in Childhood* and was influential in raising issues about the boundaries of focus groups.
mrvega@edu.ucm.es

Rolf L Wirsing has a Masters of Public Health from Berkeley, CA and a PhD in Anthropology from SUNY Buffalo, NY. After fieldwork projects in inner-city USA, the Orinocco, the Peruvian Highlands and a small town in Turkey, he was Professor of Medical Anthropology, Fachbereich Sozialwesen, Hochschule Zittau/Goerlitz, Germany. During *Living with Asthma in Childhood*, as with the two preceding projects, he coordinated the Goerlitz team and was pivotal in the planning and piloting of the focus group format. Rolf is a pensioner as of early 2008, but continues to teach anthropology at the Alice Salomon University of Applied Sciences in Berlin, pursues his research interests and was essential in formating the manuscript of this present volume.
wirsingRolf@aol.com